SRA

OPEN COURT

CLASSICS

⇸ *Program Authors* ⇷

Carl Bereiter, Ph.D.

Sandra N. Kaplan, Ed.D.

Michael Pressley, Ph.D.

SRA

A Division of The **McGraw·Hill** *Companies*

Columbus, Ohio

❖ Acknowledgments ❖

Grateful acknowledgment is given to the following publishers and copyright owners for permissions granted to reprint selections from their publications. All possible care has been taken to trace ownership and secure permission for each selection included. In case of any errors or omissions, the Publisher will be pleased to make suitable acknowledgments in future editions.

RISKS AND CONSEQUENCES
From CHARLIE AND THE CHOCOLATE FACTORY by Roald Dahl, copyright © 1964 by Roald Dahl. Copyright renewed 1992 by Felicity Dahl, Tessa Dahl, Theo Dahl, Ophelia Dahl, and Lucy Dahl. Copyright assigned to Roald Dahl Nominee Ltd 1994. Used by permission of Alfred A. Knopf Children's Books, a division of Random House, Inc. UK rights by kind permission of David Higham Associates.

"Mella: Young Friend of the Python" from WOMEN WARRIORS: MYTHS AND LEGENDS OF HEROIC WOMEN by MARIANNA MAYER. Used by permission of HarperCollins Publishers.

Excerpt from BEHIND REBEL LINES: THE INCREDIBLE STORY OF EMMA EDMONDS, CIVIL WAR SPY, copyright © 1988 by Seymour Reit, reprinted by permission of Harcourt, Inc.

DOLLARS AND SENSE
From WHERE THE RED FERN GROWS by Wilson Rawls, copyright © 1961 by Sophie S. Rawls, Trustee, or successor Trustee(s) of the Rawls Trust, dated July 31, 1991. Copyright © 1961 by The Curtis Publishing Company. Used by permission of Random House Children's Books, a division of Random House, Inc.

From THE ENDLESS STEPPE: GROWING UP IN SIBERIA by Esther Hautzig. COPYRIGHT © 1968 BY ESTHER HAUTZIG. Used by permission of HarperCollins Publishers.

FROM MYSTERY TO MEDICINE
Edel Wignell is an Australian freelance writer. "Lingering Leeches" was previously published in CRICKET MAGAZINE (USA) and in TOUCHDOWN MAGAZINE (Australia). Used by permission of the author.

Copyright © 1997 by James Herriot. From: JAMES HERRIOT'S ANIMAL STORIES by James Herriot. Reprinted by permission of St. Martin's Press, LLC.

From WHEN PLAGUE STRIKES: THE BLACK DEATH, SMALLPOX, AIDS BY JAMES CROSS GIBLIN. TEXT COPYRIGHT © 1995 BY JAMES CROSS GIBLIN. Used by permission of HarperCollins Publishers.

SURVIVAL
LETTERS FROM RIFKA by Karen Hesse, © 1992 by Karen Hesse. Reprinted by permission of Henry Holt and Company, LLC.

"Excerpts," from MY SIDE OF THE MOUNTAIN by Jean Craighead George, copyright © 1959, renewed © 1987 by Jean Craighead George. Used by permission of Dutton Children's Books, an imprint of Penguin Putnam Books for Young Readers, a division of Penguin Putnam Inc.

COMMUNICATION
From THE STORY OF DOCTOR DOLITTLE. Told by Hugh Lofting. Published by permission of the Estate of Hugh Lofting c/o Ralph M. Vicinanza, Ltd.

"Forgotten Language" from WHERE THE SIDEWALK ENDS by Shel Silverstein. COPYRIGHT © 1974 BY EVIL EYE MUSIC, INC. Used by permission of HarperCollins Publishers.

"How the Alphabet Was Made" from JUST SO STORIES by Rudyard Kipling. Reprinted with the permission of A.P. Watt Ltd. On behalf of The National Trust for Places of Historical Interest or Natural Beauty.

"Someday" by Isaac Asimov. First published in *Infinity Science Fiction*, August 1956. Published by permission of the Estate of Isaac Asimov c/o Ralph M. Vicinanza, Ltd.

A CHANGING AMERICA
From ESCAPE FROM SLAVERY: THE BOYHOOD OF FREDERICK DOUGLASS IN HIS OWN WORDS edited and illustrated by Michael McCurdy, Editorial and illustrations copyright © 1994 by Michael McCurdy. Used by permission of Alfred A. Knopf Children's Books, a division of Random House, Inc.

"Frederick Douglass" by Robert Hayden, editor. Copyright © 1966 by Robert Hayden, from COLLECTED POEMS OF ROBERT HAYDEN by Robert Hayden, edited by Frederick Glaysher. Used by permission of Liveright Publishing Corporation.

"Rails Across the Country" from A HISTORY OF US: RECONSTRUCTION AND REFORM (VOL. 7) by Joy Hakim, copyright © 1994 by Joy Hakim. Used by permission of Oxford University Press.

www.sra4kids.com

SRA/McGraw-Hill

A Division of The McGraw-Hill Companies

↦ Level 4 ↤

Risks and Consequences

✦

Dollars and Sense

✦

From Mystery to Medicine

✦

Survival

✦

Communication

✦

A Changing America

Table of Contents

UNIT
1
Risks and Consequences

 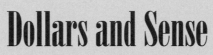

UNIT 2 — Dollars and Sense

UNIT 3 From Mystery to Medicine

UNIT 4 Survival

UNIT 5 Communication

UNIT

6

A Changing America

UNIT

1

Risks and Consequences

*First weigh the considerations,
then take the risks.*
—Helmuth von Moltke—

Good-by Violet

from **Charlie and the Chocolate Factory**
by Roald Dahl
illustrated by Doris Ettlinger

Charlie Bucket lives in a small wooden house on the edge
of town with his mother and father and his four grandparents.
The Bucket family does not have a lot of money and they are
beginning to starve. One day, as Charlie hungrily walked
home from school he found a dollar bill lying in the gutter.
He quickly ran to a nearby store and bought and devoured a
delicious Whipple-Scrumptious Fudgemallow Delight candy bar,
a chocolate candy bar made by the famous Mr. Willy Wonka.
Charlie decided to buy another one. This time, he is surprised
to discover a Golden Ticket tucked away in the candy wrapper.
Charlie is now one of the five lucky children that will tour Mr.
Willy Wonka's wonderful Chocolate Factory, see the making
of the best candy in the world, and receive a lifetime supply
of chocolate.

Once inside the factory, Charlie, Grandpa Joe, and the other
four children and their parents experience all the unknown
wonders of Mr. Willy Wonka and his candy. However, when
one of the children, Violet Beauregarde, does not listen to Mr.
Willy Wonka's warning and tries his newly invented gum, she
and the others witness a consequence they never expected.

"This gum," Mr. Wonka went on, "is my latest, my greatest, my most fascinating invention! It's a chewing-gum meal! It's . . . it's . . . it's . . . that tiny little strip of gum lying there is a whole three-course dinner all by itself!"

"What sort of nonsense is this?" said one of the fathers.

"My dear sir!" cried Mr. Wonka, "when I start selling this gum in the shops it will change *everything!* It will be the end of all kitchens and all cooking! There will be no more marketing to do! No more buying of meat and groceries! There'll be no knives and forks at mealtimes! No plates! No washing up! No garbage! No mess! Just a little strip of Wonka's magic chewing gum —and that's all you'll ever need at breakfast, lunch, and supper! This piece of gum I've just made happens to be tomato soup, roast beef, and blueberry pie, but you can have almost anything you want!"

"What *do* you mean, it's tomato soup, roast beef, and blueberry pie?" said Violet Beauregarde.

"If you were to start chewing it," said Mr. Wonka, "then that is exactly what you would get on the menu. It's absolutely amazing! You can actually *feel* the food going down your throat and into your tummy! And you can taste it perfectly! And it fills you up! It satisfies you! It's terrific!"

"It's utterly impossible," said Veruca Salt.

"Just so long as it's gum," shouted Violet Beauregarde, "just so long as it's a piece of gum and I can chew it, then *that's* for me!" And quickly she took her own world-record piece of chewing gum out of her mouth and stuck it behind her left ear. "Come on, Mr. Wonka," she said, "hand over this magic gum of yours and we'll see if the thing works."

"Now, Violet," said Mrs. Beauregarde, her mother; "don't let's do anything silly, Violet."

"I want the gum!" Violet said obstinately. "What's so silly?"

"I would rather you didn't take it," Mr. Wonka told her gently. "You see, I haven't got it *quite right* yet. There are still one or two things. . . ."

"Oh, to heck with that!" said Violet, and suddenly, before Mr. Wonka could stop her, she shot out a fat hand and grabbed the stick of gum out of the little drawer and popped it into her mouth. At once, her huge well-trained jaws started chewing away on it like a pair of tongs.

"Don't!" said Mr. Wonka.

"Fabulous!" shouted Violet. "It's tomato soup! It's hot and creamy and delicious! I can feel it running down my throat!"

"Stop!" said Mr. Wonka. "The gum isn't ready yet! It's not right!"

"Of course it's right!" said Violet. "It's working beautifully! Oh my, what lovely soup this is!"

"Spit it out!" said Mr. Wonka.

"It's changing!" shouted Violet, chewing and grinning both at the same time. "The second course is coming up! It's roast beef! It's tender and juicy! Oh boy, what a flavor! The baked potato is marvelous, too! It's got a crispy skin and it's all filled with butter inside!"

"But how *in*teresting, Violet," said Mrs. Beauregarde. "You *are* a clever girl."

"Keep chewing, kiddo!" said Mr. Beauregarde. "Keep right on chewing, baby! This is a great day for the Beauregardes! Our little girl is the first person in the world to have a chewing-gum meal!"

Everybody was watching Violet Beauregarde as she stood there chewing this extraordinary gum. Little Charlie Bucket was staring at her absolutely spellbound, watching her huge rubbery lips as they pressed and unpressed with the chewing, and Grandpa Joe stood beside him, gaping at the girl. Mr. Wonka was wringing his hands and saying, "No, no, no, no, no! It isn't ready for eating! It isn't right! You mustn't do it!"

"Blueberry pie and cream!" shouted Violet. "Here it comes! Oh my, it's perfect! It's beautiful! It's . . . it's exactly as though I'm swallowing it! It's as though I'm chewing and swallowing great big spoonfuls of the most marvelous blueberry pie in the world!"

"Good heavens, girl!" shrieked Mrs. Beauregarde suddenly, staring at Violet, "what's happening to your nose!"

"Oh, be quiet, mother, and let me finish!" said Violet.

"It's turning blue!" screamed Mrs. Beauregarde. "Your nose is turning blue as a blueberry!"

"Your mother is right!" shouted Mr. Beauregarde. "Your whole nose has gone purple!"

"What *do* you mean?" said Violet, still chewing away.

"Your cheeks!" screamed Mrs. Beauregarde. "They're turning blue as well! So is your chin! Your whole face is turning blue!"

"Spit that gum out at once!" ordered Mr. Beauregarde.

"Mercy! Save us!" yelled Mrs. Beauregarde. "The girl's going blue and purple all over! Even her hair is changing color! Violet, you're turning violet, Violet! What *is* happening to you!"

"I *told* you I hadn't got it quite right," sighed Mr. Wonka, shaking his head sadly.

"I'll say you haven't!" cried Mrs. Beauregarde. "Just look at the girl now!"

Everybody was staring at Violet. And what a terrible peculiar sight she was! Her face and hands and legs and neck, in fact the skin all over her body, as well as her great big mop of curly hair, had turned a brilliant, purplish-blue, the color of blueberry juice!

"It *always* goes wrong when we come to the dessert," sighed Mr. Wonka. "It's the blueberry pie that does it. But I'll get it right one day, you wait and see."

"Violet," screamed Mrs.
Beauregarde, "you're swelling up!"
"I feel sick," Violet said.
"You're swelling up!" screamed Mrs.
Beauregarde again.
"I feel most peculiar!" gasped Violet.
"I'm not surprised!" said Mr. Beauregarde.
"Great heavens, girl!" screeched Mrs. Beauregarde.
"You're blowing up like a balloon!"
"Like a blueberry," said Mr. Wonka.
"Call a doctor!" shouted Mr. Beauregarde.
"Prick her with a pin!" said one of the other fathers.
"Save her!" cried Mrs. Beauregarde, wringing her hands.
But there was no saving her now. Her body was swelling
up and changing shape at such a rate that within a
minute it had turned into nothing less than an
enormous round blue ball—a gigantic blueberry, in
fact—and all that remained of Violet Beauregarde
herself was a tiny pair of legs and a tiny pair
of arms sticking out of the great round
fruit and a little head on top.

"It *always* happens like that," sighed Mr. Wonka. "I've tried it twenty times in the Testing Room on twenty Oompa-Loompas, and every one of them finished up as a blueberry. It's most annoying. I just can't understand it."

"But I don't want a blueberry for a daughter!" yelled Mrs. Beauregarde. "Put her back to what she was this instant!"

Mr. Wonka clicked his fingers, and ten Oompa-Loompas appeared immediately at his side.

"Roll Miss Beauregarde into the boat," he said to them, "and take her along to the Juicing Room at once."

"The *Juicing Room?*" cried Mrs. Beauregarde. "What are they going to do to her there?"

"Squeeze her," said Mr. Wonka. "We've got to squeeze the juice out of her immediately. After that, we'll just have to see how she comes out. But don't worry, my dear Mrs. Beauregarde. We'll get her repaired if it's the last thing we do. I *am* sorry about it all, I really am. . . ."

Already the ten Oompa-Loompas were rolling the enormous blueberry across the floor of the Inventing Room toward the door that led to the chocolate river where the boat was waiting. Mr. and Mrs. Beauregarde hurried after them. The rest of the party, including little Charlie Bucket and Grandpa Joe, stood absolutely still and watched them go.

About the Author

Roald Dahl was born in South Wales on September 13, 1916 to Norwegian parents. In 1920, after the death of his father, the family moved to Kent, England. Dahl moved again four years later when he was sent to a boarding school where he studied for several years. After graduating from school, Dahl moved to East Africa to work for an oil company until the start of World War II. In 1939, Dahl enlisted in the Royal Air Force but was severely injured when his plane was shot down over Egypt. He later rejoined his squadron, and in 1941 he wrote his first book, *Over to You*. It was a collection of short stories based on his experiences in the air force. Dahl was inspired to write children's books from the made-up bedtime stories that he told his own children. Dahl wrote his first book for children in 1943, *The Gremlins*, which was followed by many more favorites like *James and the Giant Peach, Charlie and the Chocolate Factory, Danny,* and *The BFG*. Roald Dahl died on November 20, 1990 in Oxford, England.

MELLA:

Young Friend of the Python

from *Women Warriors:*
Myths and Legends of Heroic Women

by Marianna Mayer
illustrated by Shelley Johnson

This tale of young Mella's courage and later her role as tribal leader is based upon the oral history of the Buhera Ba Rowzi tribe from Zimbabwe.

In a home of reeds and fiber on the edge of the lush green forest, Mella sat upon a grass mat and held her ailing father's frail hand. He had once been the wise, strong leader of the tribe, but now he could barely lift his head. The family had offered prayers and many sacrifices for his recovery. The tribal healers tried to use their magic. They played music from their pipes and drums, but they could not rouse him. Day by day his condition worsened, and as he grew weaker, the family began to prepare for his death. All, that is, except Mella.

One night while the villagers were sleeping, Mella walked out into the forest, following the footpath to a clearing. The moon overhead shone like a golden crescent in the black velvet sky. All along the moonlight had been her guide. Now she stopped and looked up at Bomu Rambi, the merciful moon goddess.

Mella called out, "Please, Bomu Rambi, give me some sign to show what I must do to save my father."

Suddenly the wind swept through the trees, and the branches gently swayed with the mysterious presence of the goddess. All at once Mella heard the soft words of Bomu Rambi floating toward her on the wind. "You must go to the Python Healer," said the moon goddess.

Though the night was warm, Mella shivered. The Python Healer struck terror into the villagers' hearts. His cave stood at the foot of a mountain in the deepest, thickest part of the jungle, and no one dared go there. Some time ago Mella's own brothers had sought him out for their father's sake. But they had fled in horror from the entrance of the python's cave, and returned to the village so terrified that they could not speak of what they had seen.

Mella returned home, but she could not sleep. That night she made up her mind to do as the moon goddess had advised, regardless of the risk. At dawn she rose before everyone else. Quickly she gathered a few things for her journey and set out.

She traveled day and night, passing ferns higher than her head, climbing rocky hills, crossing streams, sleeping in the open. Through it all, her thoughts were only of her father, and they gave her courage to go on.

At last, with the moon just a faint sliver in the sky, Mella came upon the entrance to the cave of the Python Healer.

She sucked in her breath and stopped. For the first time fear took hold. Fighting back the wish to run, the young girl struggled to steady her voice as she called out, "Python Healer, the merciful Bomu Rambi has sent me. My name is Mella, and I come to ask for your healing power to cure my father, who is gravely ill."

The jungle fell silent. Even the birds and the crickets were still as Mella waited with only the sound of her pounding heart to listen to. Then two emerald eyes shone from the darkness of the cave, and a voice thundered out, "How is it that the bravest of your village flee from me, yet one small girl comes asking for favors? Child, are you too young to realize that I could crush you with my strangling coils?"

Mella swallowed, trying to steady her trembling. She raised her head and gazed back at the huge shadowy silhouette with its burning eyes. "I fear you, mighty healer. But I have nowhere else to go. I prayed to Bomu Rambi, and she told me to seek your help."

"Your love for your father gives you courage, little one. But are you brave enough to do what is necessary? Will you let me coil myself around you?"

Though she knew that she was making herself easy prey for the serpent, Mella quickly agreed. "If this is what you ask in return for healing my father, I will not refuse."

At the same moment the clouds gathered overhead and covered the pale light of the moon. All was blackest night as the giant python slithered out of the cave. Mella could see nothing as the sound of the serpent's hissing drew closer and closer until she could feel his breath upon her face. Slowly he rose and began to wind himself around and around her. At last only Mella's head, arms, and legs were free of the python's coils. In a hissing whisper the Python Healer told Mella to return with him to her home.

The serpent's weight was heavy, yet Mella struggled onward, following the path with her head held high. It was nightfall when they finally reached the village. When the villagers saw the monster, they ran for their weapons. But Mella called out to them, "Stop, do not harm us! You have nothing to fear. It is Mella! I have carried the Python Healer here to help my father."

Mella

Once beside the sick man, the Python Healer uncoiled, telling Mella to take healing bark and *muchonga* oil from the medicine pouch he kept hung around his neck. He instructed her to make a fire with them, and soon the vapors filled the room, giving off a sweet, smoky scent. The Python Healer began to chant, and slowly both Mella and her father fell into a restful trance.

Time passed—minutes, hours, it was impossible to say. Then the ailing man moved slowly to sit up. After a few moments longer he was on his feet. Mella could hardly believe her eyes; so many months had passed with her father scarcely able to lift his head.

"It is a miracle," cried Mella's father as he embraced his daughter. And turning to the Python Healer, he said, "Please stay with us so that I may prepare a grand celebration in your honor."

The serpent made no reply as he silently began to wrap himself around Mella once more. The young girl understood, and having said farewell to her father, she set out once more to bring the Python Healer back to his home.

When they arrived, he said, "Come into my cave."

Mella was past fear after all she had been through, and though she did not relish the idea of seeing the broken remains of victims the python had devoured, she followed him. As she went into the cave, her eyes widened with surprise at a glimmering light ahead. A few steps farther, and she saw that this light came from a mountain of shimmering golden treasure. There were baskets and baskets overflowing with gold and jewels of every color.

"You may take whatever you like," said the Python Healer, "for your courage should be rewarded."

Mella shook her head and said, "It is you who should be rewarded for healing my father."

"All the same you will take something," the python said. When Mella made no move to do so, the python said, "Here, then, I will choose for you."

Then he went to a large basket, and after a few moments he drew out a beautiful gold necklace from which hung an amulet of heavy gold cut in the shape of the crescent moon. Giving it to her, the serpent said, "You shall have the symbol of the moon goddess to remember me by. Take it, child, as a token of my friendship."

When the people of the village heard what had
happened, envy entered the hearts of three men. They
began to plot to kill the python so that they could steal his
treasure. By chance Mella overheard them scheming.
Quickly she took her bow and arrows and ran back to the
Python Healer's cave, ready to give her life if necessary
to save her friend. When the men arrived in the dead of
night, they were met by the serpent and Mella. All at once
thunder rolled, fire burst forth from the Python Healer's
magic charms, and the men fell down dead in fright.

In the years that followed, Mella lived with her father in
great happiness. And when, at last after a long full life,
Mella's father died, her people made her leader of their
tribe, for no one was more courageous or more loving
than she.

BEHIND REBEL LINES:

THE INCREDIBLE STORY OF EMMA EDMONDS, CIVIL WAR SPY

an excerpt from *Behind Rebel Lines*
by Seymour Reit
illustrated by Meg Aubrey

Sarah Emma Edmonds was born in New Brunswick in December 1841. During the 1850s, Emma left her home in Canada to move to Flint, Michigan. At the start of the Civil War in 1861, Emma enlisted as a private in the Second Michigan Infantry. Emma served in the Union army disguised as a man and used the name Franklin Thompson. While serving in the Union army, Emma was mainly a nurse and messenger. However, she was also sent on missions to spy on the Confederate army. Using a variety of disguises, such as a contraband slave named Cuff, Emma would cautiously cross Confederate lines to find out the number of the Confederate troops and their location. She would then report her findings to the Union army. After the Civil War, Emma wrote about her adventures as a soldier and spy. Some of her accounts, along with other historical documents, were used in Behind Rebel Lines.

In the following excerpt, Mrs. Butler, a chaplain's wife and friend and confidant to Emma, has disguised Emma as an Irish peddler named Bridget O'Shea. Aware of the dangers that lie ahead, Emma prepares to take another risk in order to help the Union army.

May 20, 1862

The moon was curtained with thick clouds. Wind rustled the willow trees along the Chickahominy. Now and then came the faint grumble of far-off cannon fire.

A rowboat slipped silently through the dark, pieces of blanket tied around the oars to keep them from splashing. When the boat reached the opposite river bank, a heavy middle-aged woman climbed out. She waved to the oarsman. He raised a hand in salute, turned his boat, and headed back to the far shore.

The woman, carrying a wicker basket, looked around to get her bearings. She knew from maps that the great Chickahominy swamp was on her left. If she followed its edge through the woods, she'd reach a dirt road winding away from the river. With a nod, the woman started off. Her long skirt made walking through the underbrush difficult, and branches snagged the basket she carried. After a mile or so, she found the road—a dim, gray band in the darkness. Here she would stay until dawn; then she'd head for the Confederate lines.

The tired woman sat down and leaned gratefully against a tree. Emma Edmonds, alias Franklin Thompson, alias Cuff the contraband slave, was now an Irish peddler named Bridget O'Shea. Her new disguise—and cover story—had been carefully worked out in the chaplain's cabin.

"I can't go back as Cuff," Emma had explained to Mrs. Butler. "Remember, that rebel officer left me standing guard duty. If Cuff showed up, he might be recognized. They could arrest him for deserting his post."

Mrs. Butler nodded, and the two friends lapsed into silence. Suddenly the older woman jumped up, hurried into the bedroom, and came back dragging an old campaign trunk.

"I brought a deal of fancy clothes with me from Baltimore," she said. "Lord knows I can't use them in this rough place, but *you* can."

Together they rummaged through the trunk, and soon Emma was transformed from an ordinary soldier into a plump, bosomy matron. Mrs. Butler tied a pillow around Emma's middle for bulk. Then came a petticoat, a fancy blouse, and a heavy skirt that reached the floor. Over all of this went a sweater and a fringed shawl. Mrs. Butler dusted flour in Emma's dark hair to turn it gray, then tied a big bonnet on her head. She stood back and studied the results. "One more touch," she announced. Poking in her sewing box, she found her extra pair of metal-rimmed eyeglasses and perched them on Emma's nose. "Perfect," she said. "Let them slide a bit, and look over the top."

To complete the disguise, Emma filled a basket with peddler's goods for the Southern soldiers—spools of thread, needles, matches, a pair of scissors, pieces of soap, corncakes, and packets of tea. Looking at herself in Mrs. Butler's mirror, Emma grinned. She liked the overall effect. Thousands of Irish immigrants had recently come to America, fleeing the terrible potato famine. Many had settled in this part of the country, so it was a safe cover. If anyone asked questions, she'd say she was from Providence Forge and had left a few jumps ahead of the advancing Yankees.

Now, having reached the winding road, Bridget O'Shea settled down to wait for morning. The humming of the wind made her drowsy, and she quickly dozed off. At first light she awoke, feeling stiff. The wind had risen sharply and the sky was thick with clouds; a storm was coming. Rising to her feet, Bridget twitched her skirt in place and started on her way. Fat drops of rain began to fall, making small circles in the dust. Soon the rain was coming down heavily.

The peddler trudged through the mud, trying to stay under the trees along the road. But the wind whipped the rain sideways, drenching her. Coming around a bend, she saw an old frame house up ahead. There were no lights and it appeared to be abandoned. She quietly climbed the steps, carefully opened the door, and slipped inside. The house was deserted. The floor sagged. There was no furniture and the walls were streaked with ancient dirt. Grateful to have a roof over her head, Bridget pulled off her bonnet and soggy shawl. Lord, what a downpour—what a bother.

Suddenly she froze. Someone was groaning in the next room!

Creeping to the doorway, she peeked inside. A soldier lay on the bare floor—a Confederate officer. He appeared to be no more than a boy, and she could tell he was very sick. Kneeling at his side, she touched his forehead. He was burning up, his breath coming in gasps. His pulse was weak and there were red blotches on his face. Bridget knew the symptoms—she'd seen them often enough in camp. Typhoid fever was a killer that took no sides. In both armies, the disease was doing more harm than all of the bullets, swords, and shellfire.

The young man stirred. "Water . . ."

In the kitchen, Bridget found some old crockery on a shelf. She filled a cup from the pump and hurried back to the soldier. The man drank thirstily and fell back gasping. He clutched at her hand. "Thank you, aunt."

The soldier's kit lay beside him. Bridget pulled out the blanket, folded it, and tucked it under the young man's head. Then she sat down near him. She was a firm believer in duty. Military orders were important, but this was important, too. Rebel or not, she couldn't walk away and let him die alone. She'd have to stay and keep a vigil—though she didn't think it would be for long.

All morning Bridget O'Shea sat with the dying boy. She tore a wide strip from her petticoat, and moistened it, and placed the cool pad on his forehead. He reached for her hand again. She held his hand and sang to him—old hymns and lost lullabies she dimly remembered from childhood.

There wasn't much else she could do. She gave him more water, and in the afternoon she stirred a fire in the iron stove and made tea for them both. She also shared corncakes with her companion, though he could eat little. The tea revived him briefly. He raised himself on one elbow and stared at his guardian curiously. Had he somehow seen through her disguise? Well, it didn't matter; there was nothing he could do now.

The soldier was sinking. His voice came in gasps and whispers, and bit by bit she heard his story. Allen Hall was a lieutenant in a Virginia rifle company. He'd been ill for weeks with typhoid and had tried to carry on. Two days before, at Cold Harbor, his men had fought a battle with an advance Union force. The Virginians retreated, but Hall was too sick to keep up with them. Afraid of falling into enemy hands, he'd dragged himself off through the woods, where he'd found this house and managed to crawl inside.

For a time he slipped into a coma. Later, he roused himself. "Aunt," he whispered, "if you ever pass through the Confederate camp this side of Richmond, ask for a Major McKee of General Ewell's staff. There's a gold watch in my pocket. Please give him the watch—he'll know who it should be sent to." The boy's eyes were glassy. "Tell the major—oh, just say I had a mind to go home. . . ."

Bridget O'Shea kept her vigil as the day faded into darkness. Outside, the storm raged. Rain drummed on the windows. Thunder growled. Somewhere in the house, a loose shutter went *slap . . . slap . . . slap*. And, above it all, the wind moaned, keening for dying troopers.

Bridget stood up and stretched. Her back and shoulders ached. She walked to the window, stared at nothing, and went back to her soldier. She was feeling restless and weary. The sounds of the storm—rising and falling—slowly created their own music. A new hymn was making the rounds of the Union camps—a song written only a few months before by a Boston woman named Howe. Emma had found the stanzas printed in a magazine called *The Atlantic Monthly* and she'd heard it sung around the Union campfires. The glorious words were captivating, resounding in the drumming of horses' hooves, the rattle of caisson wheels, the blare of bugles and the crash of guns. Alone with her dying soldier, she heard them again in the sounds of the wind.

He is trampling out the vintage
where the grapes of wrath are stored. . . .

Lieutenant Hall muttered in delirium. She bathed his face with a cool cloth. Sitting against the wall, she held his thin hand and willed him some of her strength.

He has loosed the fateful lightning
of His terrible swift sword. . . .

She wondered when, if ever, this fearful war would end. A friend of the Butlers had just come from Washington. He told them President Lincoln had aged ten years over the last few months.

He has sounded forth the trumpet
that shall never call retreat. . . .

Now they were dying—the fine boys of both armies—gallants Lincoln had called "the brave and early fallen."

He is sifting out the hearts of men
before His judgment seat. . . .

Darkness finally came and Bridget O'Shea slept fitfully. She dozed on and off, haunted by painful dreams. In the gray light of morning, the young man was dead.

For a while she sat there, unable to move. With an effort she roused herself, found the gold watch, and put it in her basket. Then she covered the soldier with his blanket and said a silent prayer. She'd find Major McKee for him if it was the last thing she ever did.

Gathering her belongings, Bridget left the house, closing the door gently behind her. According to her reckoning, the rebels would be several miles farther to the west. She headed slowly down the road, sidestepping the worst of the puddles. The rain had long since stopped, but her face was wet. She reached up and brushed the tears away.

Devil take this ugly war. It was brutal and cruel, yet she knew the Union had to survive. For her, that was all that mattered—it was the one thing she could believe in. She willed herself to stop thinking of young Lieutenant Hall. He was at peace now, but she still had work to do. At headquarters, Colonel Shrub had shown her the secret battle map, stuck with its colored pins. "This area is a question mark," he said, poking a stubby finger at one spot. "Your mission, Thompson, is to find out what's going on here. We *must* know what tricks they're up to."

In her mind Bridget reviewed her orders—all the details and all the dangers—and fear began to creep in. Could she really carry it off? Would the disguise work this time? Would her luck hold, or was she tempting fate?

> *Oh be swift my soul to answer him,*
> *be jubilant my feet.*
> *His day is marching on. . . .*

She brushed aside her morbid thoughts. Bother the risks. She wasn't a timid peddler woman—she was a Union soldier and proud of it.

Bridget O'Shea set her chin, wiped her nose, yanked her bonnet straight, and pushed on toward the enemy lines.

May 22, 1862

The Richmond road had numerous twists and branchings, and Bridget began to fear she'd lost her way. Suddenly a voice barked, "Halt!"

A sentry in Confederate gray stepped from the bushes and came toward her suspiciously. But as he drew near, his frown softened. What he saw was a harmless middle-aged woman, her clothes bedraggled, her face pale, her eyes red from crying. The woman explained that she had come to sell her goods in camp, but now she had another purpose. "I must find a staff officer named McKee," she said. "I have a message for him from a dying soldier."

Minutes later Miss O'Shea was bouncing along in a supply wagon pulled by an old mule. The driver helped her down outside General Ewell's headquarters, where a sympathetic aide listened to her story. "I'm to give this gold watch to Major McKee," she explained. "It was the boy's last request."

The aide shook his head. The major was out with a surveying party and wouldn't be back until afternoon. "Meanwhile," he said, "make yourself comfortable, ma'am. You're welcome to the hospitality of our camp, such as it is." He led her to a tent where some black women were hard at work cooking and washing, and beckoned to one. "Take care of this lady, Rachel," he said. "See that she's comfortable and has something to eat."

Alone with the women, Bridget sat down on an empty crate and watched. They were a lively bunch, smiling and chattering, and now and then they would steal curious glances in her direction. One of them brought her two thick slices of bread made of rice and cornmeal, and a mug of sweet cider. She learned that they were contrabands—slaves who had wandered from their farms and plantations in the confusion of the war. Some contrabands made their way north; others, like this group, had been rounded up and put to work for the Confederate army. These women did the cooking and laundering for the staff at the rebel headquarters. Like many Southern house servants, they were treated far better than the field laborers and trench diggers Cuff had met before.

Wolfing her food, Bridget studied the slaves' clothing—bandannas tied neatly around their heads, aprons hitched around long, ragged skirts—making a mental note of it. It would be a useful disguise for a future mission. Listening to the gossip, she also learned about the units stationed there, the number of troops, and the names of their officers. This time she had decided to keep information in her head instead of writing it down. It would be much safer and would be good training for her.

At first the women were a bit shy as Bridget sat with them, but gradually they relaxed. Someone started to sing, and one by one the others joined in:

> *We are climbin' Jacob's ladder,*
> *We are climbin' Jacob's ladder,*
> *We are climbin' Jacob's ladder,*
> *Soldiers of the cross. . . .*

Bridget knew the hymn well. Softly, she joined them in the final chorus.

> *We are climbin' higher, higher,*
> *We are climbin' higher, higher,*
> *We are climbin' higher, higher,*
> *Soldiers of the cross.*

She sat a while longer, thinking of a deserted house and a dying man. Then, thanking the black women, she picked up her basket and stepped out to explore the area.

To her relief, she found she could move around with complete freedom. Nobody was suspicious of a poor woman trying to peddle her basket of meager goods. In fact, she sold quite a few packets of thread and pieces of soap to the friendly troopers. She also kept her eyes and ears open, talking to the soldiers, counting the various cannons, noting the layout of the defenses. All this was stored in her head; she'd have much to report when she got back to camp . . . *if* she got back to camp. There were no exact plans for her return, but she tried not to worry about that.

Three o'clock came, and with it, Major McKee. Bridget met him, turned over the gold watch, and described what had happened. The major was saddened. He shook his head and chewed the end of his droopy mustache. "Poor Allen Hall, rest his soul," he mused. "We wondered what became of the lad. At least he didn't fall into enemy hands."

The major excused himself with a bow, hurried into the headquarters tent, and returned a minute later.

"Ma'am," he asked, "can you ride?"

Bridget nodded. "Been riding since I was a shaver, sir. Had my own farm pony back in County Clare."

McKee chewed his mustache again. "Then we'd much appreciate it if you'll grant a favor. We're right anxious to bring Lieutenant Hall's body in and give it a decent burial. If it's not imposin', you think you could guide a squad out to that old house?"

The spy's heart leapt at the prospects and possibilities opening up for her. She smiled sweetly. "I'd be right proud to take them, Major."

A fine-looking chestnut horse was led from the corral. A trooper made a step with his linked hands, and she climbed into the saddle. She usually sat her horses astride, the way men did, but just in time she remembered to sit sidesaddle, legs together in a ladylike manner. A sergeant rode up beside her and touched his cap. Behind him came the mule wagon, carrying four soldiers and a wooden coffin.

McKee gave the sergeant last-minute instructions. "We have reports of Union patrols this side of the river. Move with care, Parker, and look after this brave lady."

The party started off at last, with Bridget and the sergeant in front and the wagon following. At first she worried about finding the right way back, but soon began to recognize landmarks. As they rode along she did some more probing.

"You think the Yankees will attack soon?" she asked her companion.

Parker spat tobacco juice and grinned. "I believe so, ma'am. They'll head this way soon's they finish buildin' their bridge—but we'll be ready for 'em." He swept a hand toward the dense foliage on both sides of the river. "We're hidin' lots of heavy guns here in the woods. When the Yanks come down this road they'll march straight into an ambush. Purely won't know what hit 'em."

Miss O'Shea tried to look pleased. But she filed the alarming news in her head; it was something headquarters would certainly be glad to learn.

The rescue party took a wrong turn and had to backtrack, but they finally reached the old house. A soldier hopped from the wagon, looked inside, and reported that the body was still there under its blanket. As the men began unloading the coffin, Sergeant Parker turned to his guide. "I'd be much obliged, ma'am, if you could ride up to the next bend and kind of act as lookout. Watch for stray Yanks. If I sent one of my men, they'd shoot 'im for sure—but they'll never bother you."

Bridget's eyes lit up. "Don't you fret, Sergeant. I'll keep watch. When you're ready, just start back without me and I'll catch up."

Marveling once more at her good luck, the young spy trotted half a mile down the road and slid around the bend. Once out of sight, she swung her right leg over the pommel of the saddle, then kicked the horse into a fast canter. Horse and rider raced down the road as she put distance between herself and the rebels.

After several miles she noticed that the swamp had narrowed greatly. She could even glimpse the Chickahominy through the trees. She wheeled the chestnut sharply, plunged through the underbrush, then straight into the river. The little horse was a sturdy swimmer, strong and confident. Nearing the Union side, she tore off her bonnet and waved it to attract the pickets' attention.

In a short while, Bridget O'Shea was back at headquarters, sitting across from Colonel Shrub, telling him what she'd learned. The adjutant was delighted with her report. He also admired the chestnut horse she had ridden to safety. "He's all yours, Thompson," he said. "Add him to your collection of trophies."

Later, while changing clothes at the cabin, Emma brought Mrs. Butler up to date. Then she remembered something. "Oh, Lord!" she wailed. "I plumb forgot your lovely wicker basket. It's back at the rebel camp!"

The chaplain's wife laughed. "No matter. If you ask me, a basket for a horse is a good trade."

The women went out to look at the little chestnut tethered near the cabin, cropping grass. "He's a handsome animal, Em," said Mrs. Butler. "What are you going to name him?"

Emma grinned. "Rebel," she said.

Dollars and Sense

He does not possess Wealth, it possesses him.

He that is of Opinion Money will do every Thing, may well be suspected of doing every Thing for Money.

Beware of little Expences, a small Leak will sink a

Pay what you owe, and you'll know what's your own.
—Ben Franklin—

Where the Red Fern Grows

an excerpt from ***Where the Red Fern Grows***

by Wilson Rawls
illustrated by Frank Sofo

Wilson Rawls based his novel, Where the Red Fern Grows, *on his own experiences in the Ozark Mountains of Oklahoma. Rawls's story begins on a peaceful spring afternoon. Billy Colman is making his way home from work when the yelping and howling of fighting dogs breaks the silence. As he approaches the dogs Billy notices a redbone hound emerging from the pack. The dog is injured and scared, so Billy takes the dog home where he nurses the frightened animal back to health. That night, as he watches the dog disappear into the darkness, Billy begins to recall his boyhood in northeastern Oklahoma. He remembers how he longed for two redbone hounds of his own. Billy also remembers the disappointment of not being able to afford them.*

The dog-wanting disease never did leave me altogether. With the new work I was doing, helping Papa, it just kind of burned itself down and left a big sore on my heart. Every time I'd see a coon track down in our fields, or along the riverbanks, the old sore would get all festered up and start hurting again.

Just when I had given up all hope of ever owning a good hound, something wonderful happened. The good Lord figured I had hurt enough, and it was time to lend a helping hand.

It all started one day while I was hoeing corn down in our field close to the river. Across the river, a party of fishermen had been camped for several days. I heard the old Maxwell car as it snorted and chugged its way out of the bottoms. I knew they were leaving. Throwing down my hoe, I ran down to the river and waded across at a place called the Shannon Ford. I hurried to the camp ground.

It was always a pleasure to prowl where fishermen had camped. I usually could find things: a fish line, or a forgotten fish pole. On one occasion, I found a beautiful knife stuck in the bark of a sycamore tree, forgotten by a careless fisherman. But on that day, I found the greatest of treasures, a sportsman's magazine, discarded by the campers. It was a real treasure for a country boy. Because of that magazine, my entire life was changed.

I sat down on an old sycamore log, and started thumbing through the leaves. On the back pages of the magazine, I came to the "For Sale" section—"Dogs for Sale"—every kind of dog. I read on and on. They had dogs I had never heard of, names I couldn't make out. Far down in the right-hand corner, I found an ad that took my breath away. In small letters, it read: "Registered redbone coon hound pups—twenty-five dollars each."

The advertisement was from a kennel in Kentucky. I read it over and over. By the time I had memorized the ad, I was seeing dogs, hearing dogs, and even feeling them. The magazine was forgotten. I was lost in thought. The brain of an eleven-year-old boy can dream some fantastic dreams.

How wonderful it would be if I could have two of those pups. Every boy in the country but me had a good hound or two. But fifty dollars—how could I ever get fifty dollars? I knew I couldn't expect help from Mama and Papa.

I remembered a passage from the Bible my mother had read to us: "God helps those who help themselves." I thought of the words. I mulled them over in my mind. I decided I'd ask God to help me. There on the banks of the Illinois River, in the cool shade of the tall white sycamores, I asked God to help me get two hound pups. It wasn't much of a prayer, but it did come right from the heart.

When I left the camp ground of the fishermen, it was late. As I walked along, I could feel the hard bulge of the magazine jammed deep in the pocket of my overalls. The beautiful silence that follows the setting sun had settled over the river bottoms. The coolness of the rich, black soil felt good to my bare feet.

It was the time of day when all furried things come to life. A big swamp rabbit hopped out on the trail, sat on his haunches, stared at me, and then scampered away. A mother gray squirrel ran out on the limb of a burr oak tree. She barked a warning to the four furry balls behind her. They melted from sight in the thick green. A silent gray shadow drifted down from the top of a tall sycamore. There was a squeal and a beating of wings. I heard the tinkle of a bell in the distance ahead. I knew it was Daisy, our milk cow. I'd have to start her on the way home.

I took the magazine from my pocket and again I read the ad. Slowly a plan began to form. I'd save the money. I could sell stuff to the fishermen: crawfish, minnows, and fresh vegetables. In berry season, I could sell all the berries I could pick at my grandfather's store. I could trap in the winter. The more I planned, the more real it became. There was the way to get those pups—save my money.

I could almost feel the pups in my hands. I planned the little doghouse, and where to put it. Collars I could make myself. Then the thought came, "What could I name them?" I tried name after name, voicing them out loud. None seemed to fit. Well, there would be plenty of time for names.

Right now there was something more important—fifty dollars—a fabulous sum—a fortune—far more money than I had ever seen. Somehow, some way, I was determined to have it. I had twenty-three cents—a dime I had earned running errands for my grandpa, and thirteen cents a fisherman had given me for a can of worms.

The next morning I went to the trash pile behind the barn. I was looking for a can—my bank. I picked up several, but they didn't seem to be what I wanted. Then I saw it, an old K. C. Baking Powder can. It was perfect, long and slender, with a good tight lid. I took it down to the creek and scrubbed it with sand until it was bright and new-looking.

I dropped the twenty-three cents in the can. The coins looked so small lying there on the shiny bottom, but to me it was a good start. With my finger, I tried to measure how full it would be with fifty dollars in it.

Next, I went to the barn and up in the loft. Far back over the hay and up under the eaves, I hid my can. I had a start toward making my dreams come true—twenty-three cents. I had a good bank, safe from the rats and from the rain and snow.

All through that summer I worked like a beaver. In the small creek that wormed its way down through our fields, I caught crawfish with my bare hands, I trapped minnows with an old screen-wire trap I made myself, baited with yellow corn bread from my mother's kitchen. These were sold to the fishermen, along with fresh vegetables and roasting ears. I tore my way through the blackberry patches until my hands and feet were scratched raw and red from the thorns. I tramped the hills seeking out the huckleberry bushes. My grandfather paid me ten cents a bucket for my berries.

Once Grandpa asked me what I did with the money I earned. I told him I was saving it to buy some hunting dogs. I asked him if he would order them for me when I had saved enough. He said he would. I asked him not to say anything to my father. He promised me he wouldn't. I'm sure Grandpa paid little attention to my plans.

That winter I trapped harder than ever with the three little traps I owned. Grandpa sold my hides to fur buyers who came to his store all through the fur season. Prices were cheap: fifteen cents for a large opossum hide, twenty-five for a good skunk hide.

Little by little, the nickels and dimes added up. The old K. C. Baking Powder can grew heavy. I would heft its weight in the palm of my hand. With a straw, I'd measure from the lip of the can to the money. As the months went by, the straw grew shorter and shorter.

The next summer I followed the same routine.

"Would you like to buy some crawfish or minnows? Maybe you'd like some fresh vegetables or roasting ears."

The fishermen were wonderful, as true sportsmen are. They seemed to sense the urgency in my voice and always bought my wares. However, many was the time I'd find my vegetables left in the abandoned camp.

There never was a set price. Anything they offered was good enough for me.

A year passed. I was twelve. I was over the halfway mark. I had twenty-seven dollars and forty-six cents. My spirits soared. I worked harder.

Another year crawled slowly by, and then the great day came. The long hard grind was over. I had it—my fifty dollars! I cried as I counted it over and over.

As I set the can back in the shadowy eaves of the barn, it seemed to glow with a radiant whiteness I had never seen before. Perhaps it was all imagination. I don't know.

Lying back in the soft hay, I folded my hands behind my head, closed my eyes, and let my mind wander back over the two long years. I thought of the fishermen, the blackberry patches, and the huckleberry hills. I thought of the prayer I had said when I asked God to help me get two hound pups. I knew He had surely helped, for He had given me the heart, courage, and determination.

Early the next morning, with the can jammed deep in the pocket of my overalls, I flew to the store. As I trotted along, I whistled and sang. I felt as big as the tallest mountain in the Ozarks.

Arriving at my destination, I saw two wagons were tied up at the hitching rack. I knew some farmers had come to the store, so I waited until they left. As I walked in, I saw my grandfather behind the counter. Tugging and pulling, I worked the can out of my pocket and dumped it out in front of him and looked up.

Grandpa was dumbfounded. He tried to say something, but it wouldn't come out. He looked at me, and he looked at the pile of coins. Finally, in a voice much louder than he ordinarily used, he asked, "Where did you get all this?"

"I told you, Grandpa," I said, "I was saving my money so I could buy two hound pups, and I did. You said you would order them for me. I've got the money and now I want you to order them."

Grandpa stared at me over his glasses, and then back at the money.

"How long have you been saving this?" he asked.

"A long time, Grandpa," I said.

"How long?" he asked.

I told him, "Two years."

His mouth flew open and in a loud voice he said, "Two years!"

I nodded my head.

The way my grandfather stared at me made me uneasy. I was on needles and pins. Taking his eyes from me, he glanced back at the money. He saw the faded yellow piece of paper sticking out from the coins. He worked it out, asking as he did, "What's this?"

I told him it was the ad, telling where to order my dogs.

He read it, turned it over, and glanced at the other side.

I saw the astonishment leave his eyes and the friendly-old-grandfather look come back. I felt much better.

Dropping the paper back on the money, he turned, picked up an old turkey-feather duster, and started dusting where there was no dust. He kept glancing at me out of the corner of his eye as he walked slowly down to the other end of the store, dusting here and there.

He put the duster down, came from behind the counter, and walked up to me. Laying a friendly old work-calloused hand on my head, he changed the conversation altogether, saying "Son, you need a haircut."

I told him I didn't mind. I didn't like my hair short; flies and mosquitoes bothered me.

He glanced down at my bare feet and asked, "How come your feet are cut and scratched like that?"

I told him it was pretty tough picking blackberries barefoot.

He nodded his head.

It was too much for my grandfather. He turned and walked away. I saw the glasses come off, and the old red handkerchief come out. I heard the good excuse of blowing his nose. He stood for several seconds with his back toward me. When he turned around, I noticed his eyes were moist.

In a quavering voice, he said, "Well, Son, it's your money. You worked for it, and you worked hard. You got it honestly, and you want some dogs. We're going to get those dogs.". . .

About the Author

Wilson Rawls was born on a small farm near Scraper, Oklahoma, on September 24, 1913. His mother taught him and his sisters at home how to read and write. Rawls's dream of becoming a writer emerged after he read *The Call of the Wild* by Jack London. When the Great Depression struck, sixteen-year-old Rawls decided to leave home and find work. While traveling, Rawls began writing stories; however, his poor grammar and spelling prevented his stories from being sold. Embarrassed, Rawls burned his stories, but Sofie, his wife, encouraged him to rewrite them. After her help with spelling and grammar, the first version of *Where the Red Fern Grows* was published in the *Saturday Evening Post* in 1961. Rawls died in 1984.

The ENDLESS STEPPE:
GROWING UP IN SIBERIA

an excerpt from *The Endless Steppe*
by Esther Hautzig
illustrated by Stacey Schuett

In June of 1941, Esther Rudomin was enjoying the simple comforts of life in Poland even though Europe was at war. However, the peacefulness of her world was suddenly shattered when two Russian soldiers arrested her family for political reasons. The family was forced into a cattle car and sent on a long journey across Russia. The Rudomins soon arrived at their destination—the endless steppe of Siberia. They would spend the next five years living in exile.

In this excerpt, Esther and her grandmother have been given permission to travel into Rubtsovsk, a nearby village, and trade their belongings at an outdoor market. This story is an autobiography, the author's true story.

We received permission to go in two weeks.
When we heard that Rubtsovsk had a market, a
baracholka, where one could exchange goods for
rubles and which was open on Sunday, it was
agreed that Grandmother and I should do some
trading. *Rubles* meant food—potatoes perhaps;
anything but bread and *brinza*. We spent every
night deciding which of our few belongings we
were ready to sell. One of Mother's lace-trimmed
French silk slips went in and out of a bag a dozen
times. "I really don't need this for dynamiting
gypsum," she said.

"Nor do I need this," Father said, holding up
a custom made silk shirt, "for driving a wagon."

Grandmother wasn't so sure they wouldn't need
them, and she herself was most reluctant to part
with a black silk umbrella with a slender silver
handle.

I thought that Sunday would never
come. When it did, Grandmother
and I set off down the dusty
road before anyone else.
Along with our wares—the
slip, the shirt, and the
umbrella, after all—we had
wrapped some bread in
one of my father's
handkerchiefs; the bread
was to be our lunch.

It was shortly after six o'clock, the air was still cool and fresh, a hawk was soaring overhead, and, feeling oddly disloyal, I thought that the steppe was just a tiny bit beautiful that morning.

I glanced back over my shoulder. No one was coming after us to order us to return to the mine, but I quickened my pace and urged Grandmother to hurry.

When the mine was out of sight, when there was nothing but Grandmother and me and the steppe, nothing else, not even a hawk in the sky, I didn't shout—I wouldn't dare because of the way sound carried—I didn't sing very loud, but I sang, and my funny little voice sounded strange to me. And I felt light, as if I could do a giant leap over the steppe.

"Grandmother, do you know what?"

"What?"

"We are doing something we *want* to do. All by ourselves. We are fr-r-r-eeeee. . . ."

"Shh!" Grandmother looked around. "Not so loud."

She was dressed in her best dress, a rumpled blue silk that was also beginning to fade, and her little Garbo hat. In spite of her tininess, Grandmother had always been the *grande dame;* walking down the dusty road that day, she still was.

We walked for about three hours across the uninhabited steppe without meeting one other person. Before long, I had tied my sweater around my waist—my pleated school skirt and blouse had become my uniform—and Grandmother had opened her umbrella.

We saw a bump in the distance. This turned out to be the first of the widely scattered huts, which meant that before too long we would be in Rubtsovsk.

The village had appeared on the horizon like a mirage always receding from us, but we finally did reach it and it was real. Wonderfully real to my starved eyes.

Rubtsovsk, at that time, had an unused church with its onion top, a bank, a library, a pharmacy, a school—even a movie house and a park with a bandstand. But all I saw that day was a square alive with people and, only vaguely, a rather mean cluster of wooden buildings and huts.

We squeezed our way through the crowd—the men in peaked caps, here and there an old military cap, women in *babushkas*, friendly faces sometimes scarred from frostbite, friendly voices. And some *Kazakhs*; Asia at last! Colorful costumes, the women with their long pigtails encased in cloth and leather pouches, and, sad to see, men, women, and children all with rotting teeth. But *Kazakhs!*

Trading was going on all around us. There were the stalls around the square with produce from the collective farms—and the small farmers too—and there were the buildings with signs proclaiming them to be state-operated stores where one made purchases only if one had been issued ration books, which we had not been. In one corner, sunflower seeds were being roasted over an open fire. The smell was ravishing. "Come on, Grandmother." I nudged her. "Let's begin to trade."

We made our way to the *baracholka,* where
wooden horses were set up all over the interior of
the square and where piles of stuff were heaped
onto blankets or onto the bare stones: old boots,
jackets, *babushkas,* books, pots, pans—anything
and everything.

We found a place to stand and, to my surprise,
without feeling the least bit self-conscious I
immediately held up my mother's slip, the lacy
pink silk blowing in the breeze. In a second, we
were surrounded: Where were we from? Where did
we live? What did Grandmother do? How old was I?
They were exceedingly friendly and frankly
inquisitive, these native Siberians.

We answered the questions as fast as we could, with Grandmother doing most of the talking, since she knew Russian well and I hardly spoke it. We coaxed our potential customers to note the beauty of the lace, the fact that there were 16, *sixteen,* ribs in the umbrella. How much? Forty *rubles. Forty rubles?* There was a roar of laughter. All right, thirty-eight *rubles* . . . I caught Grandmother's eye; we smiled at each other; we were born traders and we were having a marvelous time. It was, in fact, the happiest time I had had in a long, long time. The guns, the bombs of World War II were thousands of miles away and at the market place so was the labor camp close by. All around me children were giggling over nothing, girls were showing off their dolls—what if they were made of rags?—and boys were wrestling. These children were just like the children in Vilna. Hunger, fatigue, sorrow, and fright were forgotten: haggling was a wonderfully engrossing game. Rough hands that had scrounged in the earth for potatoes, and been frostbitten more than once, fingered the silk, sometimes as if it were a rosary, sometimes as if it were sinful for anything to be that silky, more often to test it for durability. If an egg was around fifteen *rubles,* how much should a silk slip with *hand-drawn* lace be? Hand drawn, mule drawn, what difference if you couldn't eat it? We all joined in the laughter. I don't remember who bought Father's shirt and Grandmother's umbrella, but the slip was finally bought by a young woman with lots of orange rouge on her cheeks. She was so plump I wondered how she was going to squeeze into it, but that, I decided, was her worry, not mine.

Feeling very proud of ourselves with our newly acquired *rubles,* we now became the customers. What to buy? We went to the stalls where the produce was—watermelons, cucumbers, potatoes, milk, flour, *white* bread—a great luxury—and meat. Everything was incredibly expensive and we walked back and forth from stall to stall, unable to make a decision. I stood perfectly still in front of the roasting sunflower seeds, ostentatiously breathing in and out. Grandmother counted the *rubles* we had. "Come," she said, "what are grandmothers for?" The first purchase was a small glassful of sunflower seeds. I slit the shell between my teeth and extracted the tiny nut. I nursed it as if it were a piece of precious candy and it could not have tasted better. Siberians love sunflower seeds and I think ninety percent of them bore a little notch in a front tooth to prove it.

After much deliberation and more bargaining, we bought a piece of meat and a bag of flour. There was a communal outdoor stove at the schoolhouse and we could boil the meat on it and, after mixing the flour with water, we could bake little cakes, the Siberian cakes of our *Diaspora.*

By that time, the sun had begun to set and Grandmother said we must start our long hike home. But I could tell that she was as reluctant to leave this carnival as I was. So, it seemed, was everyone else. The stalls were empty of their produce; like some kind of game, everyone had everyone else's belongings, wrapped in blankets, coats, *babushkas,* old flour sacks. But having come together in this vast, lonely steppe, having joked and gossiped and even sung songs, no one wanted to leave.

However, as we began our long trudge back we were very gay, thinking only of the *baracholka,* not of the mine. Grandmother and I had this in common, we were "very" people—either very sad or very gay, with nothing in between. Oh, if we could only live in the village and go to the *baracholka* every Sunday, Siberia would be bearable. I started to tick off the things I had to sell—three dresses, one blouse, a coat . . . Grandmother laughed. "Stop before you go naked in exchange for a glassful of sunflower seeds."

No matter, I thought, whether I had something to sell or not, I would pray that one day we would be allowed to live in the village within sight and sound of the Sunday *baracholka.*

Louisa May Alcott based her best-known novel on her own experiences growing up with three sisters. In *Little Women,* the March sisters—Meg, Jo, Beth, and Amy—and their mother, Marmee, reside in Concord, Massachusetts, during the Civil War. Mr. March has joined the army, and in his absence, the family befriends their wealthy neighbor, Mr. Laurence, and his grandson, Laurie. Under the watchful eyes and guidance of Marmee and Hannah, their housekeeper, as well as the companionship of their kindly neighbors, the sisters learn to face their meager circumstances with humor, love, and courage.

In this excerpt, a dreary November day turns gloomier with the arrival of a telegram about Mr. March's condition. Although she does not have the money, Marmee must make the trip to Washington, D.C., immediately. In a flurry of activity, the family makes the necessary last-minute arrangements. Jo's sacrifice for her family is one of the most memorable scenes from this novel.

A Telegram

from **Little Women**

by Louisa May Alcott
illustrated by Jessie Willcox Smith

"November is the most disagreeable month in the whole year," said Margaret, standing at the window one dull afternoon, looking out at the frostbitten garden.

"That's the reason I was born in it," observed Jo pensively, quite unconscious of the blot on her nose.

"If something very pleasant should happen now, we should think it a delightful month," said Beth, who took a hopeful view of everything, even November.

"I dare say; but nothing pleasant ever *does* happen in this family," said Meg, who was out of sorts. "We go grubbing along day after day, without a bit of change, and very little fun. We might as well be in a treadmill."

"My patience, how blue we are!" cried Jo. "I don't much wonder, poor dear, for you see other girls having splendid times, while you grind, grind, year in and year out. Oh, don't I wish I could manage things for you as I do for my heroines! You're pretty enough and good enough already, so I'd have some rich relation leave you a fortune unexpectedly; then you'd dash out as an heiress, scorn everyone who has slighted you, go abroad, and come home my lady Something, in a blaze of splendor and elegance."

"People don't have fortunes left them in that style nowadays; men have to work, and women to marry for money. It's a dreadfully unjust world," said Meg bitterly.

"Jo and I are going to make fortunes for you all; just wait ten years, and see if we don't," said Amy, who sat in a corner, making mud pies, as Hannah called her little clay models of birds, fruit, and faces.

"Can't wait, and I'm afraid I haven't much faith in ink and dirt, though I'm grateful for your intentions."

Meg sighed, and turned to the frostbitten garden again; Jo groaned, and leaned both elbows on the table in a despondent attitude, but Amy spatted away energetically; and Beth, who sat at the other window, said, smiling, "Two pleasant things are going to happen right away: Marmee is coming down the street, and Laurie is tramping through the garden as if he had something nice to tell."

In they both came, Mrs. March with her usual question, "Any letter from father, girls?" and Laurie to say in his persuasive way, "Won't some of you come for a drive? I've been working away at mathematics till my head is in a muddle, and I'm going to freshen my wits by a brisk turn. It's a dull day, but the air isn't bad, and I'm going to take Brooke home, so it will be gay inside, if it isn't out. Come, Jo, you and Beth will go, won't you?"

"Of course we will."

"Much obliged, but I'm busy;" and Meg whisked out her workbasket, for she had agreed with her mother that it was best, for her at least, not to drive often with the young gentleman.

"We three will be ready in a minute," cried Amy, running away to wash her hands.

"Can I do anything for you, Madam Mother?" asked Laurie, leaning over Mrs. March's chair, with the affectionate look and tone he always gave her.

"No, thank you, except call at the office, if you'll be so kind, dear. It's our day for a letter, and the postman hasn't been. Father is as regular as the sun; there's some delay on the way, perhaps."

A sharp ring interrupted her, and a minute after Hannah came in with a letter.

"It's one of them horrid telegraph things, mum," she said, handing it as if she was afraid it would explode and do some damage.

At the word "telegraph," Mrs. March snatched it, read the two lines it contained, and dropped back into her chair as white as if the little paper had sent a bullet to her heart. Laurie dashed downstairs for water, while Meg and Hannah supported her, and Jo read aloud, in a frightened voice,—

"Mrs. March:
"Your husband is very ill. Come at once.
"S. Hale,
"Blank Hospital, Washington."

How still the room was as they listened breathlessly, how strangely the day darkened outside, and how suddenly the whole world seemed to change, as the girls gathered about their mother, feeling as if all the happiness and support of their lives was about to be taken from them. Mrs. March was herself again directly; read the message over, and stretched out her arms to her daughters, saying, in a tone they never forgot, "I shall go at once, but it may be too late. O children, children, help me to bear it!"

For several minutes there was nothing but the sound of sobbing in the room, mingled with broken words of comfort, tender assurances of help, and hopeful whispers that died away in tears. Poor Hannah was the first to recover, and with unconscious wisdom she set all the rest a good example; for, with her, work was the panacea for most afflictions.

"The Lord keep the dear man! I won't waste no time a cryin', but git your things ready right away, mum," she said heartily, as she wiped her face on her apron, gave her mistress a warm shake of the hand with her own hard one, and went away, to work like three women in one.

"She's right; there's no time for tears now. Be calm, girls, and let me think."

They tried to be calm, poor things, as their mother sat up, looking pale, but steady, and put away her grief to think and plan for them.

"Where's Laurie?" she asked presently, when she had collected her thoughts, and decided on the first duties to be done.

"Here, ma'am. Oh, let me do something!" cried the boy, hurrying from the next room, whither he had withdrawn, feeling that their first sorrow was too sacred for even his friendly eyes to see.

"Send a telegram saying I will come at once. The next train goes early in the morning. I'll take that."

"What else? The horses are ready; I can go anywhere, do anything," he said, looking ready to fly to the ends of the earth.

"Leave a note at Aunt March's. Jo, give me that pen and paper."

Tearing off the blank side of one of her newly copied pages, Jo drew the table before her mother, well knowing that money for the long, sad journey must be borrowed, and feeling as if she could do anything to add a little to the sum for her father.

"Now go, dear; but don't kill yourself driving at a desperate pace; there is no need of that."

Mrs. March's warning was evidently thrown away; for five minutes later Laurie tore by the window on his own fleet horse, riding as if for his life.

"Jo, run to the rooms, and tell Mrs. King that I can't come. On the way get these things. I'll put them down; they'll be needed, and I must go prepared for nursing. Hospital stores are not always good. Beth, go and ask Mr. Laurence for a couple of bottles of old wine: I'm not too proud to beg for father; he shall have the best of everything. Amy, tell Hannah to get down the black trunk; and, Meg, come and help me find my things, for I'm half bewildered."

Writing, thinking, and directing, all at once, might well bewilder the poor lady, and Meg begged her to sit quietly in her room for a little while, and let them work. Everyone scattered like leaves before a gust of wind; and the quiet, happy household was broken up as suddenly as if the paper had been an evil spell.

Mr. Laurence came hurrying back with Beth, bringing every comfort the kind old gentleman could think of for the invalid, and friendliest promises of protection for the girls during the mother's absence, which comforted her very much. There was nothing he didn't offer, from his own dressing gown to himself as escort. But that last was impossible. Mrs. March would not hear of the old gentleman's undertaking the long journey; yet an expression of relief was visible when he spoke of it, for anxiety ill fits one for traveling. He saw the look, knit his heavy eyebrows, rubbed his hands, and marched abruptly away, saying he'd be back directly. No one had time to think of him again till, as Meg ran through the entry, with a pair of galoshes in one hand and a cup of tea in the other, she came suddenly upon Mr. Brooke.

"I'm very sorry to hear of this, Miss March," he said, in the kind, quiet tone which sounded very pleasantly to her perturbed spirit. "I came to offer myself as escort to your mother. Mr. Laurence has commissions for me in Washington, and it will give me real satisfaction to be of service to her there."

Down dropped the galoshes, and the tea was very near following, as Meg put out her hand, with a face so full of gratitude, that Mr. Brooke would have felt repaid for a much greater sacrifice than the trifling one of time and comfort which he was about to make.

"How kind you all are! Mother will accept, I'm sure; and it will be such a relief to know that she has someone to take care of her. Thank you very, very much!"

Meg spoke earnestly, and forgot herself entirely till something in the brown eyes looking down at her made her remember the cooling tea, and lead the way into the parlor, saying she would call her mother.

Everything was arranged by the time Laurie returned with a note from Aunt March, enclosing the desired sum, and a few lines repeating what she had often said before,—that she had always told them it was absurd for March to go into the army, always predicted that no good would come of it, and she hoped they would take her advice next time. Mrs. March put the note in the fire, the money in her purse, and went on with her preparations, with her lips folded tightly, in a way which Jo would have understood if she had been there.

The short afternoon wore away; all the other errands were done, and Meg and her mother busy at some necessary needlework while Beth and Amy got tea, and Hannah finished her ironing with what she called a "slap and a bang," but still Jo did not come. They began to get anxious; and Laurie went off to find her, for no one ever knew what freak Jo might take into her head. He missed her, however, and she came walking in with a very queer expression of countenance, for there was a mixture of fun and fear, satisfaction and regret, in it, which puzzled the family as much as did the roll of bills she laid before her mother, saying, with a little choke in her voice, "That's my contribution towards making father comfortable and bringing him home!"

"My dear, where did you get it? Twenty-five dollars! Jo, I hope you haven't done anything rash?"

"No, it's mine honestly; I didn't beg, borrow, or steal it. I earned it! and I don't think you'll blame me, for I only sold what was my own."

As she spoke, Jo took off her bonnet, and a general outcry arose, for all her abundant hair was cut short.

"Your hair! Your beautiful hair!" "Oh Jo, how could you? Your one beauty." "My dear girl, there was no need of this." "She doesn't look like my Jo anymore, but I love her dearly for it!"

As everyone exclaimed, and Beth hugged the cropped head tenderly, Jo assumed an indifferent air, which did not deceive anyone a particle, and said, rumpling up the brown bush, and trying to look as if she liked it, "It doesn't affect the fate of the nation, so don't wail, Beth. It will be good for my vanity; I was getting too proud of my wig. It will do my brains good to have that mop taken off; my head feels deliciously light and cool, and the barber said I could soon have a curly crop, which will be boyish, becoming, and easy to keep in order. I'm satisfied; so please take the money, and let's have supper."

"Tell me all about it, Jo. *I* am not quite satisfied, but I can't blame you, for I know how willingly you sacrificed your vanity, as you call it, to your love. But, my dear, it was not necessary, and I'm afraid you will regret it, one of these days," said Mrs. March.

"No, I won't!" returned Jo stoutly, feeling much relieved that her prank was not entirely condemned.

"What made you do it?" asked Amy, who would as soon have thought of cutting off her head as her pretty hair.

"Well, I was wild to do something for father," replied Jo, as they gathered about the table, for healthy young people can eat even in the midst of trouble. "I hate to borrow as much as mother does, and I knew Aunt March would croak; she always does, if you ask for a ninepence. Meg gave all her quarterly salary toward the rent, and I only got some clothes with mine, so I felt wicked, and was bound to have some money, if I sold the nose off my face to get it."

"You needn't feel wicked, my child: you had no winter things, and got the simplest with your own hard earnings," said Mrs. March, with a look that warmed Jo's heart.

"I hadn't the least idea of selling my hair at first, but as I went along I kept thinking what I could do, and feeling as if I'd like to dive into some of the rich stores and help myself. In a barber's window I saw tails of hair with the prices marked; and one black tail, not so thick as mine, was forty dollars. It came over me all of a sudden that I had one thing to make money out of, and without stopping to think, I walked in, asked if they bought hair, and what they would give for mine."

"I don't see how you dared to do it," said Beth, in a tone of awe.

"Oh, he was a little man who looked as if he merely lived to oil his hair. He rather stared, at first, as if he wasn't used to having girls bounce into his shop and ask him to buy their hair. He said he didn't care about mine, it wasn't the fashionable color, and he never paid much for it in the first place; the work put into it made it dear, and so on. It was getting late, and I was afraid, if it wasn't done right away, that I shouldn't have it done at all, and you know when I start to do a thing, I hate to give it up; so I begged him to take it, and told him why I was in such a hurry. It was silly, I dare say, but it changed his mind, for I got rather excited, and told the story in my topsy-turvy way, and his wife heard, and said so kindly,—

"'Take it, Thomas, and oblige the young lady; I'd do as much for our Jimmy any day if I had a spire of hair worth selling.'"

"Who was Jimmy?" asked Amy, who liked to have things explained as they went along.

"Her son, she said, who was in the army. How friendly such things make strangers feel, don't they? She talked away all the time the man clipped, and diverted my mind nicely."

"Didn't you feel dreadfully when the first cut came?" asked Meg, with a shiver.

"I took a last look at my hair while the man got his things, and that was the end of it. I never snivel over trifles like that; I will confess, though, I felt queer when I saw the dear old hair laid out on the table, and felt only the short, rough ends on my head. It almost seemed as if I'd an arm or a leg off. The woman saw me look at it, and picked out a long lock for me to keep. I'll give it to you, Marmee, just to remember past glories by; for a crop is so comfortable I don't think I shall ever have a mane again."

Mrs. March folded the wavy chestnut lock, and laid it away with a short gray one in her desk. She only said "Thank you, deary," but something in her face made the girls change the subject, and talk as cheerfully as they could about Mr. Brooke's kindness, the prospect of a fine day tomorrow, and the happy times they would have when father came home to be nursed.

No one wanted to go to bed, when, at ten o'clock, Mrs. March put by the last finished job, and said, "Come, girls." Beth went to the piano, and played the father's favorite hymn; all began bravely, but broke down one by one, till Beth was left alone, singing with all her heart, for to her music was always a sweet consoler.

"Go to bed and don't talk, for we must be up early, and shall need all the sleep we can get. Goodnight, my darlings," said Mrs. March, as the hymn ended, for no one cared to try another.

They kissed her quietly, and went to bed as silently as if the dear invalid lay in the next room. Beth and Amy soon fell asleep in spite of the great trouble, but Meg lay awake, thinking the most serious thoughts she had ever known in her short life. Jo lay motionless, and her sister fancied that she was asleep, till a stifled sob made her exclaim, as she touched a wet cheek,—

"Jo, dear, what is it? Are you crying about father?"

"No, not now."

"What then?"

"My—my hair!" burst out poor Jo, trying vainly to smother her emotion in the pillow.

It did not sound at all comical to Meg, who kissed and caressed the afflicted heroine in the tenderest manner.

"I'm not sorry," protested Jo, with a choke. "I'd do it again tomorrow, if I could. It's only the vain selfish part of me that goes and cries in this silly way. Don't tell anyone, it's all over now. I thought you were asleep, so I just made a little private moan for my one beauty. How came you to be awake?"

"I can't sleep, I'm so anxious," said Meg.

"Think about something pleasant, and you'll soon drop off."

"I tried it, but felt wider awake than ever."

"What did you think of?"

"Handsome faces,—eyes particularly," answered Meg, smiling to herself, in the dark.

"What color do you like best?"

"Brown—that is, sometimes; blue are lovely."

Jo laughed, and Meg sharply ordered her not to talk, then amiably promised to make her hair curl, and fell asleep to dream of living in her castle in the air.

The clocks were striking midnight, and the rooms were very still, as a figure glided quietly from bed to bed, smoothing a coverlid here, settling a pillow there, and pausing to look long and tenderly at each unconscious face, to kiss each with lips that mutely blessed, and to pray the fervent prayers which only mothers utter. As she lifted the curtain to look out into the dreary night, the moon broke suddenly from behind the clouds, and shone upon her like a bright, benignant face, which seemed to whisper in the silence, "Be comforted, dear soul! There is always light behind the clouds."

About the Author

Louisa May Alcott was born on November 29, 1832, in Pennsylvania. At an early age, Alcott and her three sisters, Anna, Elizabeth, and May, were encouraged to read and keep diaries. Alcott quickly discovered her talent for writing and began writing poetry, plays, stories, and fables. In 1852, she sold her first story. Alcott began writing *Little Women* in 1867. She finished the book, which was basically the story of her own family, in two and a half months. When *Little Women* was published in 1868, it was an instant success. Alcott's other works include *Flower Fables, Good Wives, Little Men, Rose in Bloom,* and *Jo's Boys;* however, *Little Women* still remains her most popular work. Louisa May Alcott died in 1888.

From Mystery to Medicine

There are no such things as incurables; there are only things for which man has not found a cure.
—Bernard M. Baruch—

Lingering Leeches

by Edel Wignell

"Ugh!" I screamed. "I've got a leech on my leg!"

I scrambled out of the water, yelling and jumping about. The other children swimming with me didn't make a fuss but watched calmly. One girl came over and tugged at the leech, but it didn't let go. "Oh well," she said. "Let it suck for a while, and then it'll fall off."

As a child, I lived on a farm in Australia and swam in an irrigation channel every day in the summer. If a leech grabbed onto me, I got the horrors. I was so squeamish that the mere *thought* of a leech could ruin a swim.

An up-close look at a leech.

What is a leech exactly? Leeches are closely related to earthworms, but unlike worms, they have suckers on each end of their bodies. On land, leeches use these suckers to walk end over end, like inchworms. Leeches can be found all over the world, both on land and in water, though most live in water. The largest leeches are found in the Amazon and can grow as long as eighteen inches.

Leeches are best known for their bloodthirstiness, but not all of them are bloodsuckers. Most varieties eat small worms, snails, and insect larvae. Yet it's the bloodsucking types that have always fascinated (or grossed out) humans. A bloodsucking leech can sense heat and vibrations from people and animals passing through its habitat, so it can quickly move toward a host and attach itself with its suckers. Once it starts sucking blood, a leech can swell to five times its original size. One big meal, lasting twenty minutes or so, could sustain a leech for as long as a year, so it may not need to feed more than a few times in its two-to-six-year life span.

Two children watch curiously as a leech swims in a fishbowl.

Bloodsucking leeches have played a large role in medicine worldwide over the last two thousand years. In fact, the art of healing was once called "leechcraft." For hundreds of years, the technique of bleeding or bloodletting was believed to be an effective way to treat diseases. Bloodletting involved cutting into a patient's vein or artery and letting it bleed for a period of time. Healers eventually discovered that using leeches was a safer way of bleeding patients, since they are natural bloodsuckers, and there was less risk of infection or excessive blood loss. Leeching was prescribed to treat headaches, skin diseases, whooping cough, and even mental illness. Doctors now know that bloodletting does very little to cure most ailments and often does the patient more harm than good.

During the eighteenth and nineteenth centuries in Europe, demand for medicinal leeches skyrocketed, and several species nearly became extinct. Napoleon imported almost 6 million leeches for his army in one year, and in France over 100 million medicinal leeches were used annually. Leeches became so expensive that some pharmacies started to rent them. For a fee, customers could take leeches home, use them to treat their illnesses, and return them. But leech rental actually helped spread diseases, since the blood a leech ingested from one customer could infect another.

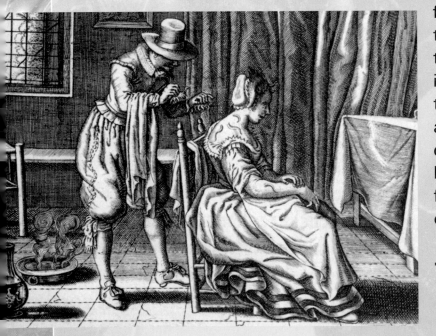

A doctor practices leechcraft by putting leeches on a patient's back in this 1624 woodcut.

Dr. Matthew Concannon displays a container of leeches.

Leeches do have a legitimate role in modern medicine. Doctors occasionally use them to help rejoined body parts heal properly. For example, let's say a person needed a toe transplanted to replace a lost thumb. This operation would involve connecting many tiny blood vessels together. The transplanted tissue (the toe) would take about a week to adapt to its new location and tap into the blood supply. During this time, the newly joined blood vessels could block up. While blood would continue to pump into the toe, there would be no way for it to drain back out. As a result pressure might build up, and the toe could become extremely painful. But if a leech were applied to the wound, it would suck up the extra blood in the toe until new veins could grow and pump out the surplus.

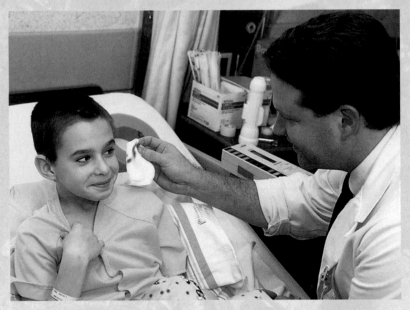

After reattaching the patient's ear, Dr. Matthew
Concannon used leeches to control the blood flow.

Leeches have proven successful in treating finger, toe,
leg, nose, and even ear transplants. In 1985 in Boston, a
five-year-old boy's ear was bitten off by a dog. During a
ten-hour operation it was rejoined, but then the ear's blood
vessels became blocked up. The boy's doctor decided to try
leeching, and two one-and-a-half-inch leeches were placed on
the ear. When the leeches finally got full and dropped off, they
had swelled to more than eight inches! After more than a
dozen leech treatments, the boy's ear was saved.

You may think that having a leech latch on to you would be
painful, but it isn't. Leeches secrete an anesthetic in their
saliva when they bite into their victim's skin. This is why
swimmers often don't notice when leeches hop on for an easy
meal. Leeches also secrete an anticoagulant or blood thinner
called *hirudin.* This substance keeps the blood from clotting
so that leeches can take in as much blood as possible. The
effectiveness of hirudin in thinning blood has led researchers
to test powdered dried leeches as a treatment for blood clots.

Scientists and doctors continue to research the beneficial qualities of leeches, and special farms have sprung up to keep them supplied with specimens. There's even a Medical Leech Museum in Charleston, South Carolina. Besides the giant Amazon leech, visitors there can see bowls used in bloodletting and ornate ceramic jars where leeches were kept before treatments.

If a leech attaches itself to you during a swim, it's usually not a good idea to pull it off. If you remove it forcibly, part of the leech could be left behind and cause an infection. My friend in Australia was right—if the leech doesn't let go after you gently squeeze it, the best thing is to let it finish feeding and fall off. And with leech anesthetic, you won't feel a thing anyway!

Doctors who practiced leechcraft used jars, similar to this one, to hold leeches.

A Spot or Two of Bother

from *Animal Stories*
by James Herriot
illustrated by Barbara McGlynn

I am never at my best in the early morning, especially the cold mornings you get in Yorkshire when a piercing wind sweeps down from the fells, finding its way inside clothing, nipping at noses and ears. It was a cheerless time, and a particularly bad time to be standing in this cobbled farmyard watching a beautiful horse dying because of my incompetence.

It had started at eight o'clock. Mr. Kettlewell telephoned as I was finishing my breakfast.

"I 'ave a fine big cart 'oss here and he's come out in spots."

"Really? What kind of spots?"

"Well, round and flat, and they're all over 'im."

"And it started quite suddenly?"

"Aye, he were right as rain last night."

"All right, I'll have a look at him right away." I nearly rubbed my hands. Urticaria. It usually cleared up spontaneously, but an injection hastened the process and I had a new antihistamine drug to try out—it was said to be specific for this sort of thing. Anyway, it was the kind of situation where it was easy for the vet to look good. A nice start to the day.

In the fifties, the tractor had taken over most of the work on the farms, but there was still a fair number of draft horses around, and when I arrived at Mr. Kettlewell's place I realized that this one was something special.

The farmer was leading him from a loose box into the yard. A magnificent Shire, all of eighteen hands, with a noble head which he tossed proudly as he paced toward me. I appraised him with something like awe, taking in the swelling curve of the neck, the deep-chested body, the powerful limbs abundantly feathered above the massive feet.

"What a wonderful horse!" I gasped. "He's enormous!"

Mr. Kettlewell smiled with quiet pride. "Aye, he's a right smasher. I only bought 'im last month. I do like to have a good 'oss about."

He was a tiny man, elderly but sprightly, and one of my favorite farmers. He had to reach high to pat the huge neck and was nuzzled in return. "He's kind, too. Right quiet."

"Ah well, it's worth a lot when a horse is good-natured as well as good-looking." I ran my hand over the typical plaques in the skin. "Yes, this is urticaria, all right."

"What's that?"

"Sometimes it's called nettle rash. It's an allergic condition. He may have eaten something unusual, but it's often difficult to pinpoint the cause."

"Is it serious?"

"Oh no. I have an injection that'll soon put him right. He's well enough in himself, isn't he?"

"Aye, right as a bobbin."

"Good. Sometimes it upsets an animal, but this fellow's the picture of health."

As I filled my syringe with the antihistamine I felt that I had never spoken truer words. The big horse radiated health and well-being.

He did not move as I gave the injection, and I was about to put my syringe away when I had another thought. I had always used a proprietary preparation for urticaria and it had invariably worked. Maybe it would be a good idea to supplement the antihistamine, just to make sure. I wanted a good, quick cure for this splendid horse.

I trotted back to my car to fetch the old standby and injected the usual dose. Again the big animal paid no attention and the farmer laughed.

"By gaw, he doesn't mind, does 'e?"

I pocketed the syringe. "No, I wish all our patients were like him. He's a grand sort."

This, I thought, was vetting at its best. An easy, trouble-free case, a nice farmer and a docile patient who was a picture of equine beauty, a picture I could have looked at all day. I didn't want to go away although other calls were waiting. I just stood there, half listening to Mr. Kettlewell's chatter about the imminent lambing season.

"Ah well," I said at length, "I must be on my way." I was turning to go when I noticed that the farmer had fallen silent.

The silence lasted for a few moments, then, "He's dotherin' a bit," he said.

I looked at the horse. There was the faintest tremor in the muscles of the limbs. It was hardly visible, but as I watched, it began to spread upward, bit by bit, until the skin over the neck, body and rump began to quiver. It was very slight, but there was no doubt it was gradually increasing in intensity.

"What is it?" said Mr. Kettlewell.

"Oh, just a little reaction. It'll soon pass off." I was trying to sound airy, but I wasn't so sure.

With agonizing slowness the trembling developed into a generalized shaking of the entire frame and this steadily increased in violence as the farmer and I stood there in silence. I seemed to have been there a long time, trying to look calm and unworried, but I couldn't believe what I was seeing. This sudden inexplicable transition—there was no reason for it. My heart began to thump and my mouth turned dry as the shaking was replaced by great shuddering spasms which racked the horse's frame, and his eyes, so serene a short while ago, started from his head in terror, while foam began to drop from his lips. My mind raced. Maybe I shouldn't have mixed those injections, but it couldn't have this fearful effect. It was impossible.

As the seconds passed, I felt I couldn't stand much more of this. The blood hammered in my ears. Surely he would start to recover soon—he couldn't get worse.

I was wrong. Almost imperceptibly the huge animal began to sway. Only a little at first, then more and more until he was tilting from side to side like a mighty oak in a gale. Oh, dear God, he was going to go down and that would be the end. And that end had to come soon. Even the cobbles seemed to shake under my feet as the great horse crashed to the ground. For a few moments he lay there, stretched on his side, his feet pedaling convulsively, then he was still.

Well, that was it. I had killed this magnificent horse. It was impossible, unbelievable that a few minutes ago that animal had been standing there in all his strength and beauty and I had come along with my clever new medicines and now there he was, dead.

What was I going to say? I'm terribly sorry, Mr. Kettlewell, I just can't understand how this happened. My mouth opened, but nothing came out, not even a croak. And, as though looking at a picture from the outside I became aware of the square of farm buildings with the dark, snow-streaked fells rising behind under a lowering sky, of the biting wind, the farmer and myself, and the motionless body of the horse.

I felt chilled to the bone and miserable, but I had to say my piece. I took a long, quavering breath and was about to speak when the horse raised his head slightly. I said nothing, nor did Mr. Kettlewell, as the big animal eased himself onto his chest, looked around him for a few seconds, then got to his feet. He shook his head, then walked across to his master. The recovery was just as quick, just as incredible, as the devastating collapse, and he showed no ill effects from his crashing fall onto the cobbled yard.

The farmer reached up and patted the horse's neck. "You know, Mr. Herriot, them spots have nearly gone!"

I went over and had a look. "That's right. You can hardly see them now."

Mr. Kettlewell shook his head wonderingly. "Aye, well, it's a wonderful new treatment. But I'll tell tha summat. I hope you don't mind me sayin' this, but," he put his hand on my arm and looked up into my face, "ah think it's just a bit drastic."

I drove away from the farm and pulled up the car in the lee of a drystone wall. A great weariness had descended upon me. This sort of thing wasn't good for me. I was getting on in years now—well into my thirties—and I couldn't stand these shocks like I used to. I tipped the driving mirror down and had a look at myself. I was a bit pale, but not as ghastly white as I felt. Still, the feeling of guilt and bewilderment persisted, and with it the recurring thought that there must be easier ways of earning a living than as a country veterinary surgeon. Twenty-four hours a day, seven days a week, rough, dirty and peppered with traumatic incidents like that near catastrophe back there. I leaned back against the seat and closed my eyes.

When I opened them a few minutes later, the sun had broken through the clouds, bringing the green hillsides and the sparkling ridges of snow to vivid life, painting the rocky outcrops with gold. I wound down the window and breathed in the cold clean air drifting down, fresh and tangy, from the moorland high above.

Peace began to steal through me. Maybe I hadn't done anything wrong with Mr. Kettlewell's horse. Maybe antihistamines did sometimes cause these reactions. Anyway, as I started the engine and drove away, the old feeling began to well up in me and within moments it was running strong: it was good to be able to work with animals in this thrilling countryside; I was lucky to be a vet in the Yorkshire Dales.

About the Author

James Herriot was born James Alfred Wight in Scotland in October 1916. His parents were musicians; however, Wight wanted to become a veterinarian. In 1939 he graduated from Glasgow Veterinary College. At first, Wight wished to treat small animals, but there were few positions for that type of practice available in Scotland. As a result, Wight found himself in a small town in Yorkshire. He began to record his veterinarian experiences in what would become five best-selling books. In 1972 *All Creatures Great and Small* was the first to be published. Wight changed his name and the city's name in his books to disguise their identities. James Wight died February 23, 1995, in his Yorkshire home.

Dr. Jenner's Marvelous Vaccine

from *When Plague Strikes:*
The Black Death, Smallpox, AIDS

by James Cross Giblin
illustrated by Jeffrey Thompson

When Edward Jenner was eight years old, he had a painful experience that he never forgot. Later, it helped inspire him to seek a safer and more efficient means of preventing smallpox.

Edward was the younger son of the rector of a little church in Berkeley, in the western English county of Gloucestershire. Both his parents died when Edward was five, and his older brother, Stephen—a minister like their father—took charge of Edward's upbringing.

Stephen was well-read and open to new scientific ideas like inoculation. So when a smallpox epidemic broke out in Gloucestershire in 1757, Stephen arranged to have his younger brother inoculated with a number of other children.

The inoculations were to be administered by a local pharmacist in a stable that he owned. First, though, the man bled Edward and the other children repeatedly over a period of six weeks—a procedure that dated to the time of the Black Death and even earlier. The pharmacist also gave the children large doses of laxatives to empty their stomachs.

At last the day for the inoculations arrived. Edward, like the other children, lay on a table while the pharmacist scratched his left arm with the tip of a knife, placed the dried scab from a smallpox victim over the cuts, and bandaged the arm. Edward could not go home afterward. Instead, he and the other children were forced to stay in the stable until the pharmacist judged they were no longer contagious.

After about a week, Edward, like most of the others in the stable, came down with a mild case of smallpox. His temperature soared and the characteristic rash appeared on his skin. Within three days, though, his temperature went down and the rash gradually faded away.

Shortly thereafter, the pharmacist told Edward he could go home to his brother. As he unlocked the stable door, the man clapped Edward on the shoulder and said he was now immune to any future attack of smallpox. But it took the boy almost a month to recover fully from the disease and the bleeding and purging that had preceded it.

From early childhood, Edward had shown an interest in nature and science. Sensing this, his brother Stephen arranged for him to become, at age thirteen, an apprentice to a physician in a nearby town. It was while helping Dr. Daniel Ludlow with his work that Edward first heard farm people say that they could not get smallpox because they had already had the cowpox.

Cowpox, a relatively mild disease of cattle, usually caused a few blisters on the udders of infected cows. Milkmaids and other farmworkers could acquire the disease when they milked sick animals. Painful sores broke out on their hands and sometimes left scars, but the disease soon passed and—unlike smallpox—was not fatal.

Young Jenner was intrigued by the stories he heard about cowpox providing its human victims with an immunity to smallpox. But Dr. Ludlow pooh-poohed them, saying there was no evidence of a connection between the two diseases.

When Edward had learned all he could locally, his brother sent him to London to study medicine with a prominent doctor there. Edward did so well that his teacher offered him a permanent position, but Edward decided he would rather return to his hometown of Berkeley to practice. In 1773 he converted a room in his brother's house into an office and set himself up as the town's only physician.

A new smallpox epidemic struck Gloucestershire in 1778. As Jenner traveled around the county giving inoculations, he was often reminded of the stories about cowpox that he had heard as a boy. Many farmworkers whom Jenner approached flatly refused to be inoculated. They told him they had already had the cowpox, and that it prevented smallpox. So there was no need to give them inoculations.

The farmworkers' stubborn resistance made Jenner think they might be right. Over the next several years, he spent much time studying cowpox. He went to one dairy farm after another, looking for cases of the disease. Some of the farmers welcomed him; others thought he was odd or maybe even a little crazy.

During his investigations, Jenner discovered that cowpox protected a person against smallpox only if he or she caught the disease when it was at its height in the infected animal. A day or two earlier or later, and the case of cowpox that resulted would be too weak to provide immunity.

He also got the idea that it might be possible, as with smallpox, to infect a person with a mild case of cowpox by inoculation. He thought this could be done first with disease-laden matter from a cow. Then matter from a sore on the infected person could be used to inoculate other humans. But it wasn't until 1796 that he was able to test his theories.

In May of that year, a local milkmaid named Sarah Nelmes cut her finger on a thorn just before milking a cow that was suffering from cowpox. Soon, a large, pus-filled sore appeared on Sarah's finger, followed by two smaller ones on her wrist.

The young woman went to Dr. Jenner for treatment, and he realized that her infection was nearing its peak. This was the chance he had been waiting for. After reassuring Sarah that she would recover, he asked her to come back in a few days, when he estimated the cowpox sores would be at their worst.

In the meantime, Dr. Jenner sought out an eight-year-old boy, James Phipps, who had never had either cowpox or smallpox. Although he could not guarantee the boy's safety, Jenner obtained the permission of James's parents to conduct an experiment on their son.

When Sarah returned to Jenner's office, James Phipps was waiting there with the doctor. First Jenner took some pus from the sore on Sarah's finger. Then, after making two small scratches on James's left arm, the doctor inserted the pus in the cuts. Afterward, he sent both James and Sarah home. There was no need for the boy to be isolated, as Jenner once had been, since cowpox could not be transmitted from one human being to another.

Jenner checked on James's condition every day. "On the ninth day," the doctor wrote, "he became a little chilly, lost his appetite, and had a headache. . . . [He] spent the night with some degree of restlessness, but on the day following he was perfectly well."

Now came the risky part of the experiment. On July 1, Jenner repeated the inoculation procedure on James Phipps, this time with matter from a smallpox patient. How would James react? Jenner thought the earlier cowpox infection would render the boy immune to the smallpox, but he couldn't be sure.

Happily, Jenner was proved right. On July 19, he reported on the results of the experiment in a letter to a friend: ". . . But now listen to the most delightful part of my story. The Boy has since been inoculated for the Smallpox which as I ventured to predict produced no [ill] effects [whatsoever]. I shall now pursue my Experiments with redoubled ardor."

The following year Jenner submitted a brief article to the Royal Society describing his experiment on James Phipps. However, it was returned to him with a note from the editors saying they found his evidence too thin. They also thought it most unlikely that anyone would believe cowpox could be used to prevent smallpox.

Jenner did not let this rejection from the Society stop him. He continued his experiments and, in 1798, inoculated five more children with cowpox. Later he followed up by inoculating three of the children with smallpox, and none of them became ill.

Jenner was now more convinced than ever that his theories were correct. He wrote a pamphlet summarizing his findings, and this time he published it himself instead of trying to go through the Royal Society. In the pamphlet, Jenner called the matter he had taken from the cowpox sore a *vaccine,* from the Latin for *obtained from a cow.* The process itself he called *vaccination,* to distinguish it from inoculation. Now the word *vaccination* is used for any immunization process that protects against a particular disease, and vaccines are obtained from many different sources.

Other English doctors read Jenner's pamphlet and conducted successful experiments of their own. Many of them published accounts that lent further support to his theories. Edward Jenner was elated. In a letter to a colleague, he predicted that "the annihilation of smallpox—the most dreadful scourge of the human race—will be the final result of [vaccination]."

The good news about vaccination traveled far beyond the borders of England. Within a few years, Jenner's pamphlet had been translated into German, French, Spanish, Dutch, and Italian. Copies of the English edition were shipped across the Atlantic to the newly independent United States.

In many places, vaccination soon replaced inoculation as the preferred method of preventing smallpox. Vaccination was simpler and cheaper than the earlier treatment, since patients did not have to remain isolated for one or two weeks after being vaccinated. It was safer, too, because cowpox was a much less severe disease.

Survival

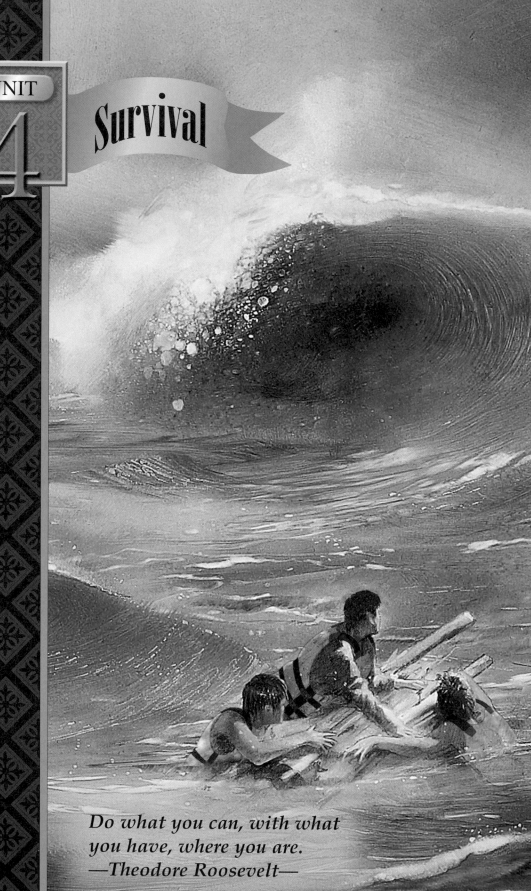

Do what you can, with what you have, where you are.
—Theodore Roosevelt—

Robinson Crusoe

an excerpt from **Robinson Crusoe**
by Daniel Defoe
retold by Edward W. Dolch, Marguerite P. Dolch,
and Beulah F. Jackson
illustrated by Doug Knutson

I Am Saved from the Sea

I was born in England in a town beside the sea. I loved the sea and when I was just a boy, I made up my mind that I was going to be a sailor.

When I grew to be a young man, I became a sailor. I had many adventures, but the one I am about to tell you was the greatest adventure of them all.

The ship I was on when this story begins was not a very large ship. There were only fourteen men on board besides the captain, his cabin boy, and myself.

We were sailing near the coast of South America. It was the time of the year when there are very bad storms in that part of the world. They are called hurricanes. All sailors are very much afraid of them.

We had been out of sight of land for many days when our captain told us to get ready for a storm. The sky grew dark and the wind began to blow very hard.

We took down the sails as fast as we could. Before we could get them rolled up, the wind blew so hard that it blew some of the sails away. The big waves began to break over the sides of our ship.

We worked as hard as we could to tie everything down to the deck of the ship. But soon, two of our men were washed overboard when a big wave caught them. The captain ordered us all to go into the cabin, for we could do nothing more.

For twelve days and twelve nights the wind and the rains and the big waves pounded our little ship. Then one morning the wind was still blowing, but not so hard. The captain and some of the sailors carefully opened the door of the cabin and went out on the deck. They had no sooner gotten outside than one man cried, "Land!"

We all ran out of the cabin to look. Just at that minute, the ship struck something and we were all thrown to the deck. A big wave broke over the ship. We had to rush back into the cabin to keep from being washed overboard.

We stood in the cabin looking at one another and thinking that our ship would break apart any minute. We did not know how much longer we had to live. Then our captain said we would try to reach land in our small boats.

On deck, we found that one of our boats had a big hole in it where the wind had driven something through it. But the other boat was still all right. We got it over the side of the ship and all of us that were left got into it.

We were not much better off there than we had been on the ship. The waves lifted us high one minute and dropped us the next. We pulled on our oars as hard as we could.

For a time we seemed to be getting nearer the land. Then a wave as high as a house lifted us, upset our boat, and before I could so much as cry out, I found myself deep in the water!

As I went down, down, down in the rough water, I thought my end had come. But I was a very strong swimmer, and I tried to save myself.

As soon as my head came out of the water, I caught a big breath. Before the next wave broke over me, I saw that I was being carried nearer the shore.

I swam as hard as I could toward the land. Wave after wave lifted me and broke over me, but at last I felt sand under my feet! As that last wave rolled back it left me on the sand so tired I could hardly move.

But I knew I could not rest until I was out of reach of the waves. I got to my feet and made myself run to a big rock. When the next wave came, I held on to the rock. The wave threw me against the rock so hard it hurt me badly. But it did not carry me back to sea. When it rolled back, I was able to run further up on the sand.

The next wave came only to my knees. Before the next one came, I was far up on the sand and came to the grass next to it. I fell down on the grass.

When I had caught my breath, I looked up and thanked God for saving my life. I was tired and hurt and wet. But I was so happy to be alive, I could hardly keep from shouting for joy. I looked out to sea. I could see our ship with the waves still breaking over her sides.

There was no sign of the other men. All of them had gone down in the sea.

Though I had been saved, I still had many troubles. I was wet and I had no dry clothes to change into. I was hungry and I had no food. I had no gun to shoot any wild beasts to eat, or to save myself in case they wanted to eat me. In short, I had nothing but what was in my pockets—a small knife, a pipe, and a little tobacco, too wet to burn.

It was growing dark. I had to do something right away, because wild beasts hunt at night.

The only thing I could think of was to get up in a tree. So I picked out a thick, bushy one which grew nearby. I saw a little stream, so first I walked to it and drank all I wanted. Then with my knife I cut a big stick. I could use it if I needed to fight.

I then climbed up in the tree and found a place where I could lie back against the branches and rest without falling out. And there I spent my first night.

I Get Back to the Ship

When I woke up the sun was shining. The storm was over. The wind had stopped. The sea was still.

Much to my surprise, our ship was still above water and was closer to shore than when I had last seen it. The wind and waves must have carried it onto a sandbar near the shore.

I made up my mind to try to swim out to the ship. I must try to get some things that I needed.

The sun was very warm when I climbed down from my tree. I put most of my clothes on the shore in the sun and swam out to the ship.

The ship lay partly on her side on the sandbar. I saw that the part of the ship where the food was stored was dry. I at once found some food, for I was hungry.

I filled my pockets with ship's bread and ate as I went over the rest of the ship. I was very happy to find the ship's dog and two cats still alive and unhurt. I made up my mind that I would try to take them to the land. They would keep me company.

The first thing I did was to make a raft. Many of the big poles to which our sails had been fastened were still on the deck. I cut these poles into shorter pieces with a carpenter's saw that I found. These I pushed over the side. I tied each one to a rope so that it would not float away. Then I let myself down into the water by a rope and I tied the poles together to make a raft. Then I tied this raft to a rope from the ship. But I found when I stood on this raft that it would not carry much weight.

I went back up the rope and took some of the boards that made the floor of the deck. I used them to make the floor of my raft. Then I got three big boxes that had belonged to some of the sailors and put them on my raft.

The thing I needed most was food. I filled one of the boxes with bread, rice, and cheese, and some dried meat.

While I was doing this, I happened to look toward the shore and saw my clothes go floating out to sea. I had not put them far enough away from the water. The tide had come in, and the water had washed them away.

I knew that I needed more clothes. I hunted until I found clothes that fit me. I put them into another of the big boxes.

I found a big box that the ship's carpenter had carried his tools in and lowered it to my raft. I knew that carpenters' tools were worth more to me than gold.

I found two good guns, two pistols, a powder horn, and a small bag of shot. I knew there was gunpowder somewhere, so I did not give up until I found three barrels of it. One was wet, and I did not know how much good it would be, but I took it anyway.

This was all my raft could carry. I called the cats, and put them on the raft. I dropped the dog into the water, and he swam ashore. I had found some oars on the ship, so I used one to paddle with. The sea was calm. The tide was running in. And a breeze blew me toward the land.

Near where I had come ashore the first time, there was a small stream running into the sea. I paddled my raft into this creek where the water was not so deep.

Here I nearly had another shipwreck. My raft caught fast on a sandbar. By working hard and fast, I was able to get the raft off the sandbar before it upset.

At last I saw a flat place where I thought I could get my raft close to the shore. I paddled as hard as I could and by pushing with my oar on the bottom of the stream, I was able to get the raft close to the land. I held it there by sticking my oar into the sand. As soon as the tide went down, my raft was safely on the land. Then I looked for a good place to put the things I had brought from the ship.

You see, I still did not know whether or not there were other people on this land. If there were other people, I did not know whether they would be friendly or whether they would try to kill me.

Neither did I know what kind of animals lived here. If there were wild animals, they might try to kill me.

Near where I had landed, there was a hill. I took one of the guns and climbed to the top of it. From that high place, I could see a long way. I did not know whether to be sad or glad about what I saw.

I saw at once that I was on a big island. There were no signs that any other people lived on the island. Far away to the west, I could see two other islands which looked smaller than mine.

There were no signs of wild animals, for which I was very thankful. The trees were full of birds, not like any that I had ever seen. I shot one of them, thinking I would eat the meat. But it had a very bad smell, so I threw it away.

I then came back to my raft and unloaded my goods. This took me the rest of the day. I put the boxes and barrels in a kind of square around a little space. I ate some of the ship's bread and cheese and drank from the stream. I lay down to sleep in the little square, with my gun beside me and the cats and dog to keep me company. I was still very much afraid, but I was so tired that I was soon fast asleep. This was the end of my first day on the island.

About the Author

Daniel Defoe was born Daniel Foe in London in 1660. He studied at an academy in London. His father had planned for him to enter the ministry. However, Daniel chose to pursue politics and trade. Around the year 1700, he changed his last name to Defoe. Many regard Defoe as the creator of the English novel. Before he began writing, most stories were written as long poems. Defoe was one of the first writers to create stories with realistic characters and situations. Defoe published his first and most famous novel, *Robinson Crusoe*, in 1719. He continued to write throughout his life, and he published other well-known books, such as *Captain Singleton* and *Moll Flanders*. Daniel Defoe died in 1731.

Letters from Rifka

an excerpt from ***Letters from Rifka***
by Karen Hesse
illustrated by Mariana Tcherepanova-Smith

Rifka is a twelve-year-old girl living in Russia in 1919 with her mama, papa, and her two brothers, Nathan and Saul. To avoid the Russian soldiers' cruel treatment of the Jews, her family makes a desperate escape from their homeland with the hope of reaching America. With no time to pack, they only grab a few treasured belongings. Rifka chooses to take a book of poetry by Alexander Pushkin. It was a gift given to her by Tovah, her favorite cousin. On the dangerous journey, Rifka carries the book and records her experiences in it as letters to Tovah.

In this excerpt, Rifka and her family have just crossed the Polish border. However, before they were allowed to enter Poland, they had to be examined for disease by rude, untrustworthy doctors who stole Mama's silver candlesticks. Rifka is devastated by the experience at the Polish border, but there is a new and bigger challenge ahead. In order to survive this challenge Rifka will have to be stronger than ever.

130

October 5, 1919
Motziv, Poland

Dear Tovah,

I thought we would be in America by now, but we remain in Poland, stranded by illness.

The sickness began with me. My legs and head started aching shortly after we crossed the Polish border.

I told Papa, "I am tired. That spray has made me sick."

By the time we arrived in Motziv my head pounded and my body hurt as if the train had run over me. I wanted only to rest. The motion of the train tormented me. I begged Papa for us to stop.

Mama and Papa took me off the train in Motziv. I did not know Papa had a cousin here, did you, Tovah? Papa's cousin did not have room for us, but he took us in anyway.

I don't remember very well what happened the first few weeks in Motziv. We slept on the floor in the shed of my father's cousin. I had dreams, terrible dreams about the guards at the train station and cossacks and entire forests chasing after me. Such nightmares!

I could not move at all. I felt imprisoned under a mound of stones.

I remember Papa down on the floor beside me, putting a damp cloth on my head. Papa is so good at nursing, but each time he placed the cloth over my eyes, I felt the weight of it crushing my head to the floor.

I tried to pull away from him, but whenever I moved, the pain exploded inside me. I begged Papa to stop, but the words would not come out. I could hardly draw a breath, there was such a heaviness on my chest.

Saul says a student of medicine came to examine me. Papa had found a student to come who spoke Russian. By then a rash had crept under my armpits and across my back and my stomach. I had a cough that threatened to split me in two each time it erupted from me.

I had typhus.

The medical student said, "Her infection started in Russia. Someone she had contact with there gave this to her."

I wanted to tell this skinny, pock-faced man that he was wrong, that my illness did not come from Russia. I knew where it started. It came from the doctor at the Polish border. I tried to explain this to the man, but I could not speak.

"You must say nothing about the nature of her illness to anyone," the medical student told Papa. "Not even to your cousin. As for the child, she will probably die. Most do. That's how it goes with typhus."

I remember very little, Tovah, but I do remember that. Those words cut through the fever and the pain. When I heard them, I wished I could die. If I died, I would be free of my suffering.

But if I died, I would never reach America.

I remember Mama crying. I tried to speak, to say I would not die, that nothing would hold me back from America, but she couldn't hear me. No one could hear me.

"I should send you all back to Russia," the medical student said. "But the child would never survive the trip."

Papa begged him to let us stay. "I promise to care for her," he said.

The medical student agreed.

I lapsed into sleep on the floor in the miserable little shed while the typhus raged inside me.

Meanwhile, Mama and Papa and Nathan grew sick. They developed the typhus too. Only Saul managed to stay healthy. Saul is too much of an ox to get sick, Tovah.

Three men took Mama and Papa and Nathan in a cart to a hospital at the other end of Motziv.

I wept to see them go. I was still so sick, but I wept to see them. As they carried Papa out and loaded him into the cart beside Mama, I thought my life was over.

"Take me too!" I cried, but I had improved compared to Mama and Papa and Nathan.

"Motziv is full of typhus," the cart driver said. "We need the beds for the dying."

They left me with Saul, of all people. Saul, who never has a kind word for me. Saul, who pulls my hair and punches me, even though Mama says at sixteen he should know better. Saul, with his big ears and his big feet, was all I had for a nurse.

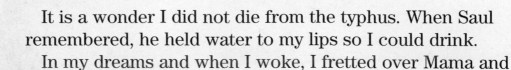

It is a wonder I did not die from the typhus. When Saul remembered, he held water to my lips so I could drink.

In my dreams and when I woke, I fretted over Mama and Papa and Nathan. Were they already dead?

"Where is Mama?" I asked each time I woke from a restless fever sleep. "Where is Papa?"

Saul turned his face away. He could not stand the smell of me; I could tell by the way his mouth tightened. "Go back to sleep, Rifka," he said. He always said the same. "Go back to sleep."

Once I woke to find Saul kneeling beside me, holding my hands down. His dark hair curled wildly around his ears. "What are you doing to yourself?" he kept asking.

I had been dreaming about Mama's candlesticks. I was holding them against my chest. Hands, dozens of hands, reached out of the darkness to take them from me. I tore at the hands, trying to get them off me, trying to get them off Mama's candlesticks.

"Look what you've done to yourself," Saul said, touching the tail of his shirt to my chest.

In my sleep, I had clawed at my chest until it bled.

Tovah, my hand is too weak to continue and my eyes blur at these tiny letters, but I will write again soon.

Shalom,

Rifka

November 3, 1919
Motziv, Poland

Dear Tovah,

I am doing much better now.

When I was well enough to move, Saul went out and found a new room for us to live in. "We cannot stay any longer in this shed," he said. Papa's family did not try to keep us from leaving. We had brought illness with us, and bad luck. We had taken from their table food they could not spare.

The room Saul found for us is in a cheap, rundown inn. The innkeeper hosts a large market outside his establishment every Wednesday. Merchants bring their wares and the innkeeper sells tea and rolls and buns. I think he makes a lot of money.

Market days are noisy. When my head aches, I cannot bear it. On my good days, though, I like to look out at the commotion.

Saul says the innkeeper is a thief, but we will stay here until Mama and Papa and Nathan are out of the hospital.

Saul found work to pay for our room and our food. He sorts apples in an orchard outside the village. At dawn, before leaving for work, Saul goes out to the street. He brings back breakfast for us, a herring and two rolls.

Each morning, when he comes with the food, Tovah, he splits it exactly in half. Even though he is bigger and needs more, he divides our food evenly.

Each day, we eat our herring and roll in a few bites and lick our fingertips to catch the crumbs. Then Saul leaves.

One day I took only a bite of my herring and decided to save the rest.

I told Saul I was not hungry.

It was a lie. I was hungry. I am hungry all the time. When I am awake, all I think about is food. When I sleep, I dream of it. My stomach twists and burns with emptiness.

But on this morning I thought, for once Saul is nice to me. I should be the same with him. Saul is working, he needs to eat more than I do. If I save my share of breakfast, it will be waiting for him in the evening when he returns.

I was still weak, but I knew I must get up and stow the herring and roll in the closet near my cot. If I did not put it away from myself, I would eat it.

My stomach knotted painfully, and in spite of my best intentions I took another bite of the herring before I closed the closet door. I hope you will not think I am too selfish, Tovah.

I turned my back on my precious food and tumbled into my cot, falling asleep immediately.

Movement in the room awakened me.

At first I thought Saul had come back, but it was not Saul. It was the girl whose father owns the inn. She sat on the edge of my cot, her thick, greasy braid hanging down her back.

She was eating something, herring and roll. The closet door was open. She was eating my herring and roll!

"Thief!" I cried in Russian. "Give me back my food!"

She ignored me. She sat on my cot, chewing.

I tried to get my roll back from her. She brushed me aside and laughed at me, Tovah.

She has so much food of her own. Always, when I see her passing by my room, she is chewing, her red cheeks swollen like a squirrel with a nut. The girl had spied on me. She had seen me save my food in the little closet and had come in and taken it for herself.

That family, they have rolls and buns all the time. It is the father's business. I drag myself from the drafty room Saul and I share and stand, swaying unsteadily in front of the bakery cases, staring at the innkeeper's food. I am so hungry, but no one offers me a crumb. The girl will be chewing, her tongue flicking out to catch a piece of bun and bring it back into her mouth again. She has all this food and she has to steal from me.

When Saul got back that evening, I told him about the girl stealing my food. I thought he would catch her and beat her up. Saul said, "Next time don't save your food, Rifka. Eat it. Then she can't take it from you."

And that was that.

With Saul gone all day, I felt lonely. Not that he was such good company, but I hated being alone, separated from Mama and Papa. In Berdichev, I could have gone to you, or to Aunt Anna, or to Bubbe Ruth.

But I was in a strange country, with no one to go to. I certainly would not go to the innkeeper's daughter, that dirty thief.

So when I grew strong enough, I started walking around Motziv. I found my way to the low, sprawling hospital where they were keeping Mama. I discovered a wooden ledge outside the window of Mama's ward and climbed on it to look in on her.

Mama lay in a narrow bed, as white as the sheet on top of her. Everything about Mama was white except her black hair. Her hair was like a dark stain on the hospital linens and her eyes remained closed, her thick lashes resting on white cheeks. She looked dead, Tovah, and I kept staring, waiting for her to move.

When the hospital workers caught me looking in at Mama, they yelled at me. They chased me away from the building. They couldn't understand that I needed to see Mama move. I needed to know she was alive. So the next day I came back, and the next day, and the next.

The Polish language has started making sense to me, Tovah. I didn't need to be clever to know I should stay out of the hospital workers' way, but I could not stay away from Mama.

Then, just this morning, a doctor caught me looking in at Mama. He did not chase me away. He lifted me down off the ledge.

"What are you doing here?" the doctor asked.

"I am watching over my mama," I explained.

The doctor asked, "Have you had the typhus?"

"Yes," I told him. "But I am better now."

The doctor said, "Come." He led me inside the hospital and sat me in a chair next to Mama's cot. "Once you have suffered through the typhus, you cannot have it again," the doctor explained. "It will do you no harm to sit with her. It may do her some good." I held Mama's hand and talked to her all the rest of today.

I even got to eat a potato out of the big pot brought by a lady who feeds the hospital patients.

They were good potatoes, Tovah. Since I have been sick, everything tastes good. How skinny I've become. But not Saul; he is as big as a horse. His legs have grown so long just since we left Russia. You should see how they sprout from his pants.

Even with all my things on, my underwear and my two extra dresses, and my cloak and shawl, I still do not look fat. Remember how in Berdichev the Russian guards would come to inspect the homes of the Jews? They made certain we owned no more than our allowance. Always, when the guards were coming, Mama would say, "Rifka, put all your clothes on." I would rush and throw my dresses over my head and stand out in front of the house to watch.

The guards would search through our rooms. They did not find more than two of anything. How could they find anything extra in our house? In your house there are many fine things, Tovah, but they never inspected your house.

The guards would look at me, layered in all my belongings, and say, "Hmmm, fat kid." With my dresses and my cloak and my shawl piled on top of me, I looked as short and round as a barrel.

I am no longer round, but I am still short. I wonder if I will ever grow, Tovah. Maybe it will be all right that I am short in America. If I could get Bubbe Ruth to come, there would at least be two of us.

If I could get Bubbe Ruth to come. She does not stay because she is comfortable and safe like you and Hannah and Uncle Avrum. Bubbe Ruth stays because she is afraid to leave, afraid for things to change. I am afraid too, but not so afraid that I want to come back.

I would like it best if you and Hannah and Uncle Avrum and Aunt Anna and Bubbe Ruth and all the others were coming to America too. I am trying to be clever, Tovah, but how much more clever I could be surrounded by my family.

Shalom, my cousin,

Rifka

About the Author

Karen Hesse was born in Baltimore, Maryland, on August 29, 1952. While in elementary school, Hesse began writing every day. She enjoyed expressing her ideas and feelings through writing. After graduating from high school, Hesse attended the University of Maryland, where she studied theater, anthropology, psychology, and English. Hesse published her first book, *Wish on a Unicorn*, in 1991. Since then she has written several other award-winning books including *Out of the Dust*, which was awarded the Newbery Medal in 1998. Karen Hesse lives in Vermont with her husband and two children.

In Which
I Have a Good Look at Winter and Find Spring in the Snow

from ***My Side of the Mountain***
written and illustrated by Jean Craighead George

With only a penknife, a ball of cord, an ax, some flint and steel, and forty dollars, Sam Gribley leaves his home and family in the city to live deep in the woods of the Catskill Mountains. In the woods, Sam must rely on the natural resources around him to survive the life-threatening elements of this majestic mountain range.

In this excerpt from My Side of the Mountain, *Sam has been living in a hollowed-out tree with Frightful, a falcon he tamed for a companion. Over the summer and fall months, Sam has successfully used the great outdoors to fill his needs for food, shelter, and clothing. However, the winter months are quickly approaching and Sam will soon be faced with the dangerous winter storms that attack the mountains. Sam's instincts and ability to live off the land will be even more valuable during these uncertain months if he wants to survive until spring.*

In Which I Have a Good Look at Winter
and Find Spring in the Snow

I lived close to the weather. It is surprising how you watch it when you live in it. Not a cloud passed unnoticed, not a wind blew untested. I knew the moods of the storms, where they came from, their shapes and colors. When the sun shone, I took Frightful to the meadow and we slid down the mountain on my snapping-turtle-shell sled. She really didn't care much for this.

When the winds changed and the air smelled like snow, I would stay in my tree, because I had gotten lost in a blizzard one afternoon and had had to hole up in a rock ledge until I could see where I was going. That day the winds were so strong I could not push against them, so I crawled under the ledge; for hours I wondered if I would be able to dig out when the storm blew on. Fortunately I only had to push through about a foot of snow. However, that taught me to stay home when the air said "snow." Not that I was afraid of being caught far from home in a storm, for I could find food and shelter and make a fire anywhere, but I had become as attached to my hemlock house as a brooding bird to her nest. Caught out in the storms and weather, I had an urgent desire to return to my tree, even as The Baron Weasel returned to his den, and the deer to their copse. We all had our little "patch" in the wilderness. We all fought to return there.

My Side of the Mountain
signed *S. Gribley*

147

I usually came home at night with the nuthatch that roosted in a nearby sapling. I knew I was late if I tapped the tree and he came out. Sometimes when the weather was icy and miserable, I would hear him high in the tree near the edge of the meadow, yanking and yanking and flicking his tail, and then I would see him wing to bed early. I considered him a pretty good barometer, and if he went to his tree early, I went to mine early too. When you don't have a newspaper or radio to give you weather bulletins, watch the birds and animals. They can tell when a storm is coming. I called the nuthatch "Barometer," and when he holed up, I holed up, lit my light, and sat by my fire whittling or learning new tunes on my reed whistle. I was now really into the

teeth of winter, and quite fascinated by its activity. There is no such thing as a "still winter night." Not only are many animals running around in the creaking cold, but the trees cry out and limbs snap and fall, and the wind gets caught in a ravine and screams until it dies. One noisy night I put this down:

"There is somebody in my bedroom. I can hear small exchanges of greetings and little feet moving up the wall. By the time I get to my light all is quiet.

"Next Day

"There was something in my room last night, a small tunnel leads out from my door into the snow. It is a marvelous tunnel, neatly packed, and it goes from a dried fern to a clump of moss. Then it turns and disappears. I would say mouse.

"That Night

"I kept an ember glowing and got a light fast before the visitor could get to the door. It was a mouse—a perfect little white-footed deer mouse with enormous black eyes and tidy white feet. Caught in the act of intruding, he decided not to retreat, but came toward me a few steps. I handed him a nut meat. He took it in his fragile paws, stuffed it in his cheek, flipped, and went out his secret tunnel. No doubt the tunnel leads right over to my store tree, and this fellow is having a fat winter."

There were no raccoons or skunks about in the snow, but the mice, the weasels, the mink, the foxes, the shrews, the cottontail rabbits were all busier than Coney Island in July. Their tracks were all over the mountain, and their activities ranged from catching each other to hauling various materials back to their dens and burrows for more insulation.

By day the birds were a-wing. They got up late, after I did, and would call to each other before hunting. I would stir up my fire and think about how much food it must take to keep one little bird alive in that fierce cold. They must eat and eat and eat, I thought.

Once, however, I came upon a male cardinal sitting in a hawthorn bush. It was a miserable day, gray, damp, and somewhere around the zero mark. The cardinal wasn't doing anything at all—just sitting on a twig, all fluffed up to keep himself warm. Now there's a wise bird, I said to myself. He is conserving his energy, none of this flying around looking for food and wasting effort. As I watched him, he shifted his feet twice, standing on one and pulling the other up into his warm feathers. I had often wondered why birds' feet didn't freeze, and there was my answer. He even sat down on both of them and let his warm feathers cover them like socks.

"January 8

"I took Frightful out today. We went over to the
meadow to catch a rabbit for her; as we passed one
of the hemlocks near the edge of the grove, she pulled
her feathers to her body and looked alarmed. I tried to
find out what had frightened her, but saw nothing.

"On the way back we passed the same tree and I
noticed an owl pellet cast in the snow. I looked up.
There were lots of limbs and darkness, but I could not
see the owl. I walked around the tree; Frightful stared
at one spot until I thought her head would swivel
off. I looked, and there it was, looking like a broken
limb—a great horned owl. I must say I was excited
to have such a neighbor. I hit the tree with a stick
and he flew off. Those great wings—they must have
been five feet across—beat the wind, but there was
no sound. The owl steered down the mountain through
the tree limbs, and somewhere not far away he
vanished in the needles and limbs.

"It is really very special to have a horned owl. I
guess I feel this way because he is such a wilderness
bird. He needs lots of forest and big trees, and so his
presence means that the Gribley farm is a beautiful
place indeed."

One week the weather gave a little to the sun, and snow melted and limbs dumped their loads and popped up into the air. I thought I'd try to make an igloo. I was cutting big blocks of snow and putting them in a circle. Frightful was dozing with her face in the sun, and the tree sparrows were raiding the hemlock cones. I worked and hummed, and did not notice the gray sheet of cloud that was sneaking up the mountain from the northwest. It covered the sun suddenly. I realized the air was damp enough to wring. I could stay as warm as a bug if I didn't get wet, so I looked at the drab mess in the sky, whistled for Frightful, and started back to the tree. We holed up just as Barometer was yanking his way home, and it was none too soon. It drizzled, it misted, it sprinkled, and finally it froze. The deer-hide door grew stiff with ice as darkness came, and it rattled like a piece of tin when the wind hit it.

I made a fire, the tree room warmed, and I puttered
around with a concoction I call possum sop. A meal
of frozen possum stewed with lichens, snakeweed,
and lousewort. It is a different sort of dish. Of course
what I really like about it are the names of all the
plants with the name possum. I fooled for an hour
or so brewing this dish, adding this and that, when
I heard the mouse in his tunnel. I realized he was
making an awful fuss, and decided it was because he
was trying to gnaw through ice to get in. I decided to
help him. Frightful was on her post, and I wanted to
see the mouse's face when he found he was in a den
with a falcon. I pushed the deerskin door. It wouldn't
budge. I kicked it. It gave a little, cracking like china,
and I realized that I was going to be iced in if I didn't
keep that door open.

I finally got it open. There must have been an inch
and a half of ice on it. The mouse, needless to say,
was gone. I ate my supper and reminded myself to
awaken and open the door off and on during the
night. I put more wood on the fire, as it was damp
in spite of the flames, and went to bed in my
underwear and suit.

I awoke twice and kicked open the door. Then I fell into a sound sleep that lasted hours beyond my usual rising time. I overslept, I discovered, because I was in a block of ice, and none of the morning sounds of the forest penetrated my glass house to awaken me. The first thing I did was try to open the door; I chipped and kicked and managed to get my head out to see what had happened. I was sealed in. Now, I have seen ice storms, and I know they can be shiny and glassy and treacherous, but this was something else. There were sheets of ice binding the aspens to earth and cementing the tops of the hemlocks in arches. It was inches thick! Frightful winged out of the door and flew to a limb, where she tried to perch. She slipped, dropped to the ground, and skidded on her wings and undercoverts to a low spot where she finally stopped. She tried to get to her feet, slipped, lost her balance, and spread her wings. She finally flapped into the air and hovered there until she could locate a decent perch. She found one close against the bole of the hemlock. It was ice free.

I laughed at her, and then I came out and took a step. I landed with an explosion on my seat. The jolt splintered the ice and sent glass-covered limbs clattering to earth like a shopful of shattering crystal. As I sat there, and I didn't dare to move because I might get hurt, I heard an enormous explosion. It was followed by splintering and clattering and smashing. A maple at the edge of the meadow had literally blown up. I feared now for my trees—the ice was too heavy to bear. While down, I chipped the deer flap clean, and sort of swam back into my tree, listening to trees exploding all over the mountain. It was a fearful and dreadful sound. I lit a fire, ate smoked fish and dried apples, and went out again. I must say I toyed with the idea of making ice skates. However, I saw the iron wagon axle iced against a tree, and crawled to it. I de-iced it with the butt of my ax, and used it for a cane. I would stab it into the ground and inch along. I fell a couple of times but not as hard as that first time.

Frightful saw me start off through the woods, for I had to see this winter display, and she winged to my shoulder, glad for a good perch. At the meadow I looked hopefully for the sun, but it didn't have a chance. The sky was as thick as Indiana bean soup. Out in the open I watched one tree after another splinter and break under the ice, and the glass sparks that shot into the air and the thunder that the ice made as it shattered were something to remember.

At noon not a drip had fallen, the ice was as tight as it had been at dawn. I heard no nuthatches, the chickadees called once, but were silent again. There was an explosion near my spring. A hemlock had gone. Frightful and I crept back to the tree. I decided that if my house was going to shatter, I would just as soon be in it. Inside, I threw sticks to Frightful and she caught them in her talons. This is a game we play when we are tense and bored. Night came and the ice still lay in sheets. We slept to the occasional boom of breaking trees, although the explosions were not as frequent. Apparently the most rotted and oldest trees had collapsed first. The rest were more resilient, and unless a wind came up, I figured the damage was over.

At midnight a wind came up. It awakened me, for the screech of the iced limbs rubbing each other and the snapping of the ice were like the sounds from a madhouse. I listened, decided there was nothing I could do, buried my head under the deer hide, and went back to sleep.

Around six or seven I heard Barometer, the nuthatch. He yanked as he went food hunting through the hemlock grove. I jumped up and looked out. The sun had come through, and the forest sparkled and shone in cruel splendor.

That day I heard the *drip, drip* begin, and by evening some of the trees had dumped their loads and were slowly lifting themselves to their feet, so to speak. The aspens and birch trees, however, were still bent like Indian bows.

Three days later, the forest arose, the ice melted, and for about a day or so we had warm, glorious weather.

The mountain was a mess. Broken trees, fallen limbs were everywhere. I felt badly about the ruins until I thought that this had been happening to the mountain for thousands of years and the trees were still there, as were the animals and birds. The birds were starved, and many had died. I found their cold little bodies under bushes and one stiff chickadee in a cavity. Its foot was drawn into its feathers, its feathers were fluffed.

Frightful ate old frozen muskrat during those days. We couldn't kick up a rabbit or even a mouse. They were in the snow under the ice, waiting it out. I suppose the mice went right on tunneling to the grasses and the mosses and had no trouble staying alive, but I did wonder how The Baron Weasel was doing. I needn't have. Here are some notes about him.

"I should not have worried about The Baron Weasel; he appeared after the ice storm, looking sleek and pleased with himself. I think he dined royally on the many dying animals and birds. In any event, he was full of pep and ran up the hemlock to chase Frightful off her perch. That Baron! It's a good thing I don't have to tie Frightful much anymore, or he would certainly try to kill her. He still attacks me, more for the fun of being sent sprawling out into the snow than for food, for he hasn't put his teeth in my trousers for months."

January was a fierce month. After the ice storm
came more snow. The mountaintop was never free of
it, the gorge was blocked; only on the warmest days
could I hear, deep under the ice, the trickle of water
seeping over the falls. I still had food, but it was
getting low. All the fresh-frozen venison was gone,
and most of the bulbs and tubers. I longed for just
a simple dandelion green.

dandelion

Toward the end of January I began to feel tired,
and my elbows and knees were a little stiff. This
worried me. I figured it was due to some vitamin
I wasn't getting, but I couldn't remember which
vitamin it was or even where I would find it if I
could remember it.

One morning my nose bled. It frightened me a bit, and I wondered if I shouldn't hike to the library and reread the material on vitamins. It didn't last long, however, so I figured it wasn't too serious. I decided I would live until the greens came to the land, for I was of the opinion that since I had had nothing green for months, that was probably the trouble.

On that same day Frightful caught a rabbit in the meadow. As I cleaned it, the liver suddenly looked so tempting that I could hardly wait to prepare it. For the next week, I craved liver and ate all I could get. The tiredness ended, the bones stopped aching and I had no more nosebleeds. Hunger is a funny thing. It has a kind of intelligence all its own. I ate liver almost every day until the first plants emerged, and I never had any more trouble. I have looked up vitamins since. I am not surprised to find that liver is rich in vitamin C. So are citrus fruits and green vegetables, the foods I lacked. Wild plants like sorrel and dock are rich in this vitamin. Even if I had known this at that time, it would have done me no good, for they were both roots in the earth. As it turned out, liver was the only available source of vitamin C—and on liver I stuffed, without knowing why.

So much for my health. I wonder now why I didn't have more trouble than I did, except that my mother worked in a children's hospital during the war, helping to prepare food, and she was conscious of what made up a balanced meal. We heard a lot about it as kids, so I was not unaware that my winter diet was off balance.

After that experience, I noticed things in the forest that I hadn't paid any attention to before. A squirrel had stripped the bark off a sapling at the foot of the meadow, leaving it gleaming white. I pondered when I saw it, wondering if he had lacked a vitamin or two and had sought them in the bark. I must admit I tried a little of the bark myself, but decided that even if it was loaded with vitamins, I preferred liver.

I also noticed that the birds would sit in the sun when it favored our mountain with its light, and I, being awfully vitamin minded at the time, wondered if they were gathering vitamin D. To be on the safe side, in view of this, I sat in the sun too when it was out. So did Frightful.

My notes piled up during these months, and my
journal of birch bark became a storage problem.
I finally took it out of my tree and cached it under
a rock ledge nearby. The mice made nests in it, but
it held up even when it got wet. That's one thing
about using the products of the forest. They are
usually weatherproof. This is important when the
weather is as near to you as your skin and as much
a part of your life as eating.

I was writing more about the animals now and less
about myself, which proves I was feeling pretty safe.
Here is an interesting entry.

"February 6

"The deer have pressed in all around me. They are
hungry. Apparently they stamp out yards in the
valleys where they feed during the dawn and dusk,
but many of them climb back to the hemlock grove
to hide and sleep for the day. They manage the deep
snows so effortlessly on those slender hooves. If I were
to know that a million years from today my children's
children's children were to live as I am living in these
mountains, I should marry me a wife with slender feet
and begin immediately to breed a race with hooves,
that the Catskill children of the future might run
through the snows and meadows and marshes as
easily as the deer."

I got to worrying about the deer, and for many days I climbed trees and cut down tender limbs for them. At first only two came, then five, and soon I had a ring of large-eyed white-tailed deer waiting at my tree at twilight for me to come out and chop off limbs. I was astonished to see this herd grow, and wondered what signals they used to inform each other of my services. Did they smell fatter? Look more contented? Somehow they were able to tell their friends that there was a free lunch on my side of the mountain, and more and more arrived.

One evening there were so many deer that I decided to chop limbs on the other side of the meadow. They were cutting up the snow and tearing up the ground around my tree with their pawing.

Three nights later they all disappeared. Not one deer came for limbs. I looked down the valley, and in the dim light could see the open earth on the land below. The deer could forage again. Spring was coming to the land! My heart beat faster. I think I was trembling. The valley also blurred. The only thing that can do that is tears, so I guess I was crying.

That night the great horned owls boomed out across the land. My notes read:

"February 10

"I think the great horned owls have eggs! The mountain is white, the wind blows, the snow is hard packed, but spring is beginning in their hollow maple. I will climb it tomorrow.

"February 12

"Yes, yes, yes, yes. It is spring in the maple. Two great horned owl eggs lie in the cold snow-rimmed cavity in the broken top of the tree. They were warm to my touch. Eggs in the snow. Now isn't that wonderful? I didn't stay long, for it is bitter weather and I wanted the female to return immediately. I climbed down, and as I ran off toward my tree I saw her drift on those muffled wings of the owl through the limbs and branches as she went back to her work. I crawled through the tunnel of ice that leads to my tree now, the wind beating at my back. I spent the evening whittling and thinking about the owl high in the forest with the first new life of the spring."

And so with the disappearance of the deer, the hoot of the owl, the cold land began to create new life. Spring is terribly exciting when you are living right in it.

I was hungry for green vegetables, and that night as I went off to sleep, I thought of the pokeweeds, the dandelions, the spring beauties that would soon be pressing up from the earth.

About the Author and Illustrator

Jean Craighead George was born in Washington D.C., in 1919. By the time George was in third grade, she was writing down her observations of animal behavior after family camping trips. George graduated from Pennsylvania State University with degrees in literature and science, and in the 1940s she worked as a reporter for *The Washington Post*. In 1959, George wrote her first book, *My Side of the Mountain*, which became a Newbery Honor Book. A sequel, *On the Far Side of the Mountain*, followed in 1990. George has written more than 60 books. Many of her books, such as *Julie of the Wolves*— a Newbery Medal winner in 1973, *Water Sky*, and *The Talking Earth*, explore the relationships between humans and animals. George researches the animals she writes about by observation and reading.

UNIT

5

Communication

The difference between the right word and the almost right word is the difference between lightning and lightning bug.
—*Mark Twain*—

Animal Language

from *The Story of Doctor Dolittle*

by Hugh Lofting

illustrated by Pat Paris

In a small town called Puddleby-on-the-Marsh lives a doctor named John Dolittle. The doctor is well-liked by all the people in the little town, but fewer and fewer people are coming to him when they are sick. Doctor Dolittle loves animals, and he shares his small house on the edge of town with rabbits, mice, chickens, pigeons, cows, horses, and several other pets. Two of his favorite pets are Jip, his dog, and Polynesia the parrot. Not all his patients are as fond of animals as he is. As a result, many travel to distant towns to visit other doctors when they are sick. Doctor Dolittle slowly loses all his patients but one: Cat's-meat-Man, who doesn't get sick very often. So, what can become of a doctor who has no patients?

It happened one day that the Doctor was sitting in
his kitchen talking with the Cat's-meat-Man who
had come to see him with a stomach-ache.

"Why don't you give up being a people's doctor, and
be an animal-doctor?" asked the Cat's-meat-Man.

The parrot, Polynesia, was sitting in the window
looking out at the rain and singing a sailor-song to
herself. She stopped singing and started to listen.

169

"You see, Doctor," the Cat's-meat-Man went on, "you know all about animals—much more than what these here vets do. That book you wrote—about cats, why, it's wonderful! I can't read or write myself—or maybe *I'd* write some books. But my wife, Theodosia, she's a scholar, she is. And she read your book to me. Well, it's wonderful—that's all can be said— wonderful. You might have been a cat yourself. You know the way they think. And listen: you can make a lot of money doctoring animals. Do you know that? You see, I'd send all the old women who had sick cats or dogs to you. And if they didn't get sick fast enough, I could put something in the meat I sell 'em to make 'em sick, see?"

"Oh, no," said the Doctor quickly. "You mustn't do that, that wouldn't be right."

"Oh, I didn't mean real sick," answered the Cat's-meat-Man. "Just a little something to make them droopy-like was what I had reference to. But as you say, maybe it ain't quite fair on the animals. But they'll get sick anyway, because the old women always give 'em too much to eat. And look, all the farmers round about who had lame horses and weak lambs—they'd come. Be an animal-doctor."

When the Cat's-meat-Man had gone the parrot flew off the window on to the Doctor's table and said:

"That man's got sense. That's what you ought to do. Be an animal-doctor. Give the silly people up—if they haven't brains enough to see you're the best doctor in the world. Take care of animals instead—they'll soon find it out. Be an animal-doctor."

"Oh, there are plenty of animal-doctors," said John Dolittle, putting the flower-pots outside on the window-sill to get the rain.

"Yes, there are plenty," said Polynesia. "But none of them are any good at all. Now listen, Doctor, and I'll tell you something. Did you know that animals can talk?"

"I knew that parrots can talk," said the Doctor.

"Oh, we parrots can talk in two languages—people's language and bird-language," said Polynesia proudly. "If I say, 'Polly wants a cracker,' you understand me. But hear this: *Ka-ka oi-ee, fee-fee*?"

"Good gracious!" cried the Doctor. "What does that mean?"

"That means, 'Is the porridge hot yet?'—in bird-language."

"My! You don't say so!" said the Doctor. "You never talked that way to me before."

"What would have been the good?" said Polynesia, dusting some cracker-crumbs off her left wing. "You wouldn't have understood me if I had."

172

"Tell me some more," said the Doctor, all excited; and he rushed over to the dresser-drawer and came back with the butcher's book and a pencil. "Now don't go too fast—and I'll write it down. This is interesting—very interesting—something quite new. Give me the birds' A.B.C. first—slowly now."

So that was the way the Doctor came to know that animals had a language of their own and could talk to one another. And all that afternoon, while it was raining, Polynesia sat on the kitchen table giving him bird words to put down in the book.

At tea-time, when the dog, Jip, came in, the parrot said to the Doctor, "See, *he's* talking to you."

"Looks to me as though he were scratching his ear," said the Doctor.

"But animals don't always speak with their mouths," said the parrot in a high voice, raising her eyebrows. "They talk with their ears, with their feet, with their tails—with everything. Sometimes they don't *want* to make a noise. Do you see now the way he's twitching up one side of his nose?"

"What's that mean?" asked the Doctor.

"That means, 'Can't you see that it's stopped raining?'" Polynesia answered. "He is asking you a question. Dogs nearly always use their noses for asking questions."

After a while, with the parrot's help, the Doctor got to learn the language of the animals so well that he could talk to them himself and understand everything they said. Then he gave up being a people's doctor altogether.

As soon as the Cat's-meat-Man had told everyone that John Dolittle was going to become an animal-doctor, old ladies began to bring him their pet pugs and poodles who had eaten too much cake; and farmers came many miles to show him sick cows and sheep.

One day a plow horse was brought to him; and the poor thing was terribly glad to find a man who could talk in horse-language.

"You know, Doctor," said the horse, "that vet over the hill knows nothing at all. He has been treating me six weeks now—for spavins. What I need is *spectacles*. I am going blind in one eye. There's no reason why horses shouldn't wear glasses, the same as people. But that stupid man over the hill never even looked at my eyes. He kept on giving me big pills. I tried to tell him; but he couldn't understand a word of horse-language. What I need is spectacles."

"Of course—of course," said the Doctor. "I'll get you some at once."

"I would like a pair like yours," said the horse— "only green. They'll keep the sun out of my eyes while I'm plowing the Fifty-Acre Field."

"Certainly," said the Doctor. "Green ones you shall have."

"You know, the trouble is, Sir," said the plow horse as the Doctor opened the front door to let him out— "the trouble is that *anybody* thinks he can doctor animals—just because the animals don't complain. As a matter of fact it takes a much cleverer man to be a really good animal-doctor than it does to be a people's doctor. My farmer's boy thinks he knows all about horses. I wish you could see him—his face is so fat he looks as though he had no eyes—and he has got as much brain as a potato-bug. He tried to put a mustard-plaster on me last week."

"Where did he put it?" asked the Doctor.

"Oh, he didn't put it anywhere—on me," said the horse. "He only tried to. I kicked him into the duck-pond."

"Well, well!" said the Doctor.

"I'm a pretty quiet creature as a rule," said the horse—"very patient with people—don't make much fuss. But it was bad enough to have that vet giving me the wrong medicine. And when that red-faced booby started to monkey with me, I just couldn't bear it any more."

"Did you hurt the boy much?" asked the Doctor.

"Oh, no," said the horse. "I kicked him in the right place. The vet's looking after him now. When will my glasses be ready?"

"I'll have them for you next week," said the Doctor. "Come in again Tuesday—Good morning!"

Then John Dolittle got a fine, big pair of green spectacles; and the plow horse stopped going blind in one eye and could see as well as ever.

And soon it became a common sight to see farm-animals wearing glasses in the country round Puddleby; and a blind horse was a thing unknown.

And so, in a few years' time, every living thing for miles and miles got to know about John Dolittle, M.D. And the birds who flew to other countries in the winter told the animals in foreign lands of the wonderful doctor of Puddleby-on-the-Marsh, who could understand their talk and help them in their troubles. In this way he became famous among the animals—all over the world—better known even than he had been among the folks of the West Country. And he was happy and liked his life very much.

About the Author

Hugh Lofting was born on January 14, 1886, in Maidenhead, England. As a child, Lofting was interested in books and writing; however, he studied civil engineering and architecture in college. After finishing his studies, Lofting traveled and worked in many different places like Africa, the West Indies, and Canada before moving to New York in 1912. Lofting lived in the United States until World War I. During the war, Lofting joined the British army and served as an officer in the Irish Guards. While Lofting served in the war, he began writing Doctor Dolittle stories. The stories began as illustrated letters that he sent to his children back in the United States. On his journey home, Lofting met a journalist who suggested publishing the stories as a book. *The Story of Doctor Dolittle* first appeared in 1920 and was the first in the *Doctor Dolittle* series. Lofting then wrote one Doctor Dolittle book every year until 1927. His stories have been translated into almost every language. In 1923 his second book, *The Voyages of Doctor Dolittle,* won the Newbery Medal. Hugh Lofting died on September 26, 1947, in Santa Monica, California.

Forgotten Language

from *Where the Sidewalk Ends*
by Shel Silverstein

Once I spoke the language of the flowers,
Once I understood each word the caterpillar said,
Once I smiled in secret at the gossip of the starlings,
And shared a conversation with the housefly
　　　　　in my bed.
Once I heard and answered all the questions
　　　　　of the crickets,
And joined the crying of each falling dying
　　　　　flake of snow,
Once I spoke the language of the flowers. . . .
　　　　How did it go?
　　　　How did it go?

About the Author

Shel Silverstein was born in Chicago, Illinois, on September 25, 1932. Although best known for his poems and stories for young readers, Silverstein also drew cartoons and composed music. Silverstein began writing and drawing cartoons as a young boy and soon developed a unique writing style that would be enjoyed by both children and adults. Silverstein continued to write and illustrate books until his death on May 10, 1999. Many of Silverstein's books, including *Where the Sidewalk Ends, Falling Up, A Light in the Attic,* and *The Giving Tree,* won awards and praise from readers and literature experts alike.

Just So Stories, by Rudyard Kipling, is a collection of stories that examines the many mysteries of the world and offers clever and out-of-the-ordinary explanations. The mysteries Kipling explores range anywhere from particular animal traits to communication between humans.

In "How the Alphabet Was Made," Taffimai, called Taffy, has just experienced the effects of what can happen when miscommunication occurs between people. With the help of her father, Tegumai, Taffy discovers a game that could unfold the secrets to written communication.

How the Alphabet Was Made

from ***Just So Stories***
by Rudyard Kipling
illustrations based on original drawings by Rudyard Kipling

The week after Taffimai Metallumai (we will still call her Taffy, Best Beloved) made that little mistake about her Daddy's spear and the Stranger-man and the picture-letter and all, she went carp-fishing again with her Daddy. Her Mummy wanted her to stay at home and help hang up hides to dry on the big drying-poles outside their Neolithic Cave, but Taffy slipped away down to her Daddy quite early, and they fished. Presently she began to giggle, and her Daddy said, 'Don't be silly, child.'

'But wasn't it inciting!' said Taffy. 'Don't you remember how the Head Chief puffed out his cheeks, and how funny the nice Stranger-man looked with the mud in his hair?'

'Well do I,' said Tegumai. 'I had to pay two deerskins—soft ones with fringes—to the Stranger-man for the things we did to him.'

'*We* didn't do anything,' said Taffy. 'It was Mummy and the other Neolithic ladies—and the mud.'

'We won't talk about that,' said her Daddy. 'Let's have lunch.'

Taffy took a marrow-bone and sat mousy-quiet for ten whole minutes, while her Daddy scratched on pieces of birch-bark with a shark's tooth. Then she said, 'Daddy, I've thinked of a secret surprise. You make a noise—any sort of noise.'

'Ah!' said Tegumai. 'Will that do to begin with?'

'Yes,' said Taffy. 'You look just like a carp-fish with its mouth open. Say it again, please.'

'Ah! ah! ah!' said her Daddy. 'Don't be rude, my daughter.'

'I'm not meaning rude, really and truly,' said Taffy. 'It's part of my secret-surprise-think. *Do* say *ah*, Daddy, and keep your mouth open at the end, and lend me that tooth. I'm going to draw a carp-fish's mouth wide-open.'

'What for?' said her Daddy.

'Don't you see?' said Taffy, scratching away on the bark. 'That will be our little secret s'prise. When I draw a carp-fish with his mouth open in the smoke at the back of our Cave—if Mummy doesn't mind—it will remind you of that ah-noise. Then we can play that it was me jumped out of the dark and s'prised you with that noise—same as I did in the beaver-swamp last winter.'

'Really?' said her Daddy, in the voice that grown-ups use when they are truly attending. 'Go on, Taffy.'

'Oh bother!' she said. 'I can't draw all of a carp-fish, but I can draw something that means a carp-fish's mouth. Don't you know how they stand on their heads rooting in the mud? Well, here's a pretence carp-fish (we can play that the rest of him is drawn). Here's just his mouth, and that means *ah*.' And she drew this. (1.)

1.

'That's not bad,' said Tegumai, and scratched on
his own piece of bark for himself; 'but you've
forgotten the feeler that hangs across his mouth.'

'But I can't draw, Daddy.'

'You needn't draw anything of him
except just the opening of his mouth
and the feeler across. Then we'll
know he's a carp-fish, 'cause the
perches and trouts haven't got
feelers. Look here, Taffy.'
And he drew this. (2.)

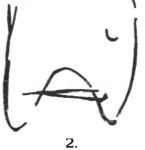

2.

'Now I'll copy it,' said Taffy.
'Will you understand *this*
when you see it?'
And she drew this. (3.)

'Perfectly,' said her Daddy.
'And I'll be quite as s'prised
when I see it anywhere, as
if you had jumped out from
behind a tree and said "Ah!" '

3.

'Now, make another noise,' said Taffy, very proud.

'Yah!' said her Daddy, very loud.

'H'm,' said Taffy. 'That's a mixy noise. The end part is *ah*-carp-fish-mouth; but what can we do about the front part? *Yer-yer-yer* and *ah! Ya!*'

'It's very like the carp-fish-mouth noise. Let's draw another bit of the carp-fish and join 'em,' said her Daddy. *He* was quite incited too.

'No. If they're joined, I'll forget. Draw it separate. Draw his tail. If he's standing on his head the tail will come first. 'Sides, I think I can draw tails easiest,' said Taffy.

'A good notion,' said Tegumai. 'Here's a carp-fish tail for the *yer*-noise.' And he drew this. (4.)

'I'll try now,' said Taffy. ''Member I can't draw like you, Daddy. Will it do if I just draw the split part of the tail, and a sticky-down line for where it joins?' And she drew this. (5.)

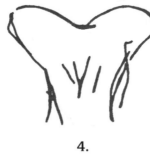

4.

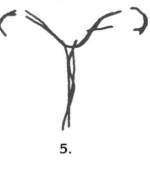

5.

Her Daddy nodded, and his eyes were shiny bright with 'citement.

'That's beautiful,' she said. 'Now, make another noise, Daddy.'

'Oh!' said her Daddy, very loud.

'That's quite easy,' said Taffy. 'You make your mouth all round like an egg or a stone. So an egg or a stone will do for that.'

'You can't always find eggs or stones. We'll have to scratch a round something like one.' And he drew this. (6.)

6.

'My gracious!' said Taffy, 'what a lot of noise-pictures we've made, –carp-mouth, carp-tail, and egg! Now, make another noise, Daddy.'

'Ssh!' said her Daddy, and frowned to himself, but Taffy was too incited to notice.

'That's quite easy,' she said, scratching on the bark.

'Eh, what?' said her Daddy. 'I meant I was thinking, and didn't want to be disturbed.'

'It's a noise, just the same. It's the noise a snake makes, Daddy, when it is thinking and doesn't want to be disturbed. Let's make the *ssh*-noise a snake. Will this do?' And she drew this. (7.)

7.

'There,' she said. 'That's another s'prise-secret. When you draw a hissy-snake by the door of your little back-cave where you mend the spears, I'll know you're thinking hard; and I'll come in most mousy-quiet. And if you draw it on a tree by the river when you're fishing, I'll know you want me to walk most *most* mousy-quiet, so as not to shake the banks.'

'Perfectly true,' said Tegumai. 'And there's more in this game than you think. Taffy, dear, I've a notion that your Daddy's daughter has hit upon the finest thing that there ever was since the Tribe of Tegumai took to using shark's teeth instead of flints for their spear-heads. I believe we've found out *the* big secret of the world.'

'Why?' said Taffy, and her eyes shone too with incitement.

'I'll show,' said her Daddy. 'What's water in the Tegumai language?'

'*Ya*, of course, and it means river too—like Wagai-*ya*—the Wagai river.'

'What is bad water that gives you fever if you drink it—black water— swamp-water?'

'*Yo*, of course.'

'Now look,' said her Daddy. 'S'pose you saw this scratched by the side of a pool in the beaver-swamp?' And he drew this. (8.)

8.

188

'Carp-tail and round egg. Two noises mixed! *Yo*, bad water,' said Taffy. ''Course I wouldn't drink that water because I'd know you said it was bad.'

'But I needn't be near the water at all. I might be miles away, hunting, and still—'

'And *still* it would be just the same as if you stood there and said, "G'way, Taffy, or you'll get fever." All that in a carp-fish-tail and a round egg! O, Daddy, we must tell Mummy, quick!' and Taffy danced all round him.

'Not yet,' said Tegumai; 'not till we've gone a little further. Let's see. *Yo* is bad water, but *so* is food cooked on the fire, isn't it?' And he drew this. (9.)

9.

'Yes. Snake and egg,' said Taffy.

'So that means dinner's ready. If you saw that scratched on a tree you'd know it was time to come to the Cave. So'd I.'

'My Winkie!' said Tegumai. 'That's true too. But wait a minute. I see a difficulty. *So* means "come and have dinner," but *sho* means the drying-poles where we hang our hides.'

'Horrid old drying-poles!' said Taffy. 'I hate helping to hang heavy, hot, hairy hides on them. If you drew the snake and egg, and I thought it meant dinner, and I came in from the wood and found that it meant I was to help Mummy hang the hides on the drying-poles, what *would* I do?'

'You'd be cross. So'd Mummy. We must make a new picture for *sho*. We must draw a spotty snake that hisses *sh-sh,* and we'll play that the plain snake only hisses *ssss.'*

'I couldn't be sure how to put in the spots,' said Taffy. 'And p'raps if *you* were in a hurry you might leave them out, and I'd think it was *so* when it was *sho*, and then Mummy would catch me just the same. *No!* I think we'd better draw a picture of the horrid high drying-poles their very selves, and make *quite* sure. I'll put 'em in just after the hissy-snake. Look!' And she drew this. (10.)

10.

'P'raps that's safest. It's very like our drying-poles, anyhow,' said her Daddy, laughing. 'Now I'll make a new noise with a snake and drying-pole sound in it. I'll say *shi*. That's Tegumai for spear, Taffy.' And he laughed.

'Don't make fun of me,' said Taffy, as she thought of her picture-letter and the mud in the Stranger-man's hair. '*You* draw it, Daddy.'

'We won't have beavers or hills this time, eh?' said her Daddy. 'I'll just draw a straight line for my spear.' And he drew this. (11.)

11.

'Even Mummy couldn't mistake that for me being killed.'

'*Please* don't, Daddy. It makes me uncomfy. Do some more noises. We're getting on beautifully.'

'Er-hm!' said Tegumai, looking up. 'We'll say *shu.* That means sky.'

Taffy drew the snake and the drying-pole. Then she stopped. 'We must make a new picture for that end sound, mustn't we?'

'*Shu-shu-u-u-u!*' said her Daddy. 'Why, it's just like the round-egg-sound made thin.'

'Then s'pose we draw a thin round egg, and pretend it's a frog that hasn't eaten anything for years.'

'N-no,' said her Daddy. 'If we drew that in a hurry we might mistake it for the round egg itself. *Shu-shu-shu!* I'll tell you what we'll do. We'll open a little hole at the end of the round egg to show how the O-noise runs out all thin, *ooo-oo-oo*. Like this.' And he drew this. (12.)

'Oh, that's lovely! Much better than a thin frog. Go on,' said Taffy, using her shark's tooth.

12.

Her Daddy went on drawing, and his hand shook with incitement. He went on till he had drawn this. (13.)

13.

'Don't look up, Taffy,' he said. 'Try if you can make out what that means in the Tegumai language. If you can, we've found the Secret.'

'Snake—pole–broken-egg—carp-tail and carp-mouth,' said Taffy. '*Shu-ya*. Sky-water (rain).' Just then a drop fell on her hand, for the day had clouded over. 'Why, Daddy, it's raining. Was *that* what you meant to tell me?'

'Of course,' said her Daddy. 'And I told it you without saying a word, didn't I?'

'Well, I *think* I would have known it in a minute, but that raindrop made me quite sure. I'll always remember now. *Shu-ya* means rain, or "it is going to rain." Why, Daddy!' She got up and danced round him. 'S'pose you went out before I was awake, and drawed *shu-ya* in the smoke on the wall, I'd know it was going to rain and I'd take my beaver-skin hood. Wouldn't Mummy be surprised!'

Tegumai got up and danced. (Daddies didn't mind doing those things in those days.) 'More than that! More than that!' he said. 'S'pose I wanted to tell you it wasn't going to rain much and you must come down to the river, what would we draw? Say the words in Tegumai-talk first.'

'*Shu-ya-las, ya maru.* (Sky-water ending. River come to.) *What* a lot of new sounds! *I* don't see how we can draw them.'

'But I do—but I do!' said Tegumai. 'Just attend a minute, Taffy, and we won't do any more today. We've got *shu-ya* all right, haven't we? But this *las* is a teaser. *La-la-la!*' and he waved his shark-tooth.

'There's the hissy-snake at the end and the carp-mouth before the snake—*as-as-as*. We only want *la-la*,' said Taffy.

'I know it, but we have to make *la-la*. And we're the first people in all the world who've ever tried to do it, Taffimai!'

'Well,' said Taffy, yawning, for she was rather tired. '*Las* means breaking or finishing as well as ending, doesn't it?'

'So it does,' said Tegumai. '*Ya-las* means that there's no water in the tank for Mummy to cook with—just when I'm going hunting, too.'

'And *shi-las* means that your spear is broken. If I'd only thought of *that* instead of drawing silly beaver-pictures for the Stranger-man!'

'*La! La! La!*' said Tegumai, waving his stick and frowning. 'Oh, bother!'

'I could have drawn *shi* quite easily,' Taffy went on. 'Then I'd have drawn your spear all broken—this way!' And she drew. (14.)

14.

'The very thing,' said Tegumai. 'That's *la* all over. It isn't like any of the other marks, either.' And he drew this. (15.)

15.

'Now for *ya*. Oh, we've done that before. Now for *maru*. *Mum-mum-mum. Mum* shuts one's mouth up, doesn't it? We'll draw a shut mouth like this.' And he drew. (16.)

16.

'Then the carp-mouth open. That makes *Ma-ma-ma!* But what about this *rrrrr*-thing, Taffy?'

'It sounds all rough and edgy, like your shark-tooth saw when you're cutting out a plank for the canoe,' said Taffy.

'You mean all sharp at the edges, like this?' said Tegumai. And he drew. (17.)

''Xactly,' said Taffy. 'But we don't want all those teeth: only put two.'

'I'll only put in one,' said Tegumai. 'If this game of ours is going to be what I think it will, the easier we make our sound-pictures the better for everybody.' And he drew. (18.)

17.

18.

'*Now* we've got it,' said Tegumai, standing on one leg. 'I'll draw 'em all in a string like fish.'

'Hadn't we better put a little bit of stick or something between each word, so's they won't rub up against each other and jostle, same as if they were carps?'

'Oh, I'll leave a space for that,' said her Daddy. And very incitedly he drew them all without stopping, on a big new bit of birch-bark. (19.)

SHU Ya LaS Ya MaRU

19.

'*Shu-ya-las-ya-maru,*' said Taffy, reading it out sound by sound.

'That's enough for today,' said Tegumai. 'Besides, you're getting tired, Taffy. Never mind, dear. We'll finish it all tomorrow, and then we'll be remembered for years and years after the biggest trees you can see are all chopped up for firewood.'

So they went home, and all that evening Tegumai sat on one side of the fire and Taffy on the other, drawing *ya's* and *yo's* and *shu's* and *shi's* in the smoke on the wall and giggling together till her Mummy said, 'Really, Tegumai, you're worse than my Taffy.'

'Please don't mind,' said Taffy. 'It's only our secret-s'prise, Mummy dear, and we'll tell you all about it the very minute it's done; but *please* don't ask me what it is now, or else I'll have to tell.'

So her Mummy most carefully didn't; and bright and early next morning Tegumai went down to the river to think about new sound-pictures, and when Taffy got up she saw *Ya-las* (water is ending or running out) chalked on the side of the big stone water-tank, outside the Cave.

'Um,' said Taffy. 'These picture-sounds are rather a bother! Daddy's just as good as come here himself and told me to get more water for Mummy to cook with.' She went to the spring at the back of the house and filled the tank from a bark bucket, and then she ran down to the river and pulled her Daddy's left ear—the one that belonged to her to pull when she was good.

'Now come along and we'll draw all the left-over sound-pictures,' said her Daddy, and they had a most inciting day of it, and a beautiful lunch in the middle, and two games of romps. When they came to T, Taffy said that as her name, and her Daddy's, and her Mummy's all began with that sound, they should draw a sort of family group of themselves holding hands. That was all very well to draw once or twice; but when it came to drawing it six or seven times, Taffy and Tegumai drew it scratchier and scratchier, till at last the T-sound was only a thin long Tegumai with his arms out to hold Taffy and Teshumai. You can see from these three pictures partly how it happened. (20, 21, 22.)

20.   21.   22.

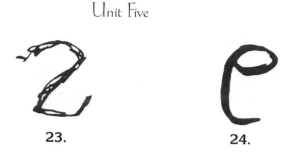

23.   24.

Many of the other pictures were much too beautiful to begin with, especially before lunch; but as they were drawn over and over again on birch-bark, they became plainer and easier, till at last even Tegumai said he could find no fault with them. They turned the hissy-snake the other way round for the Z-sound, to show it was hissing backwards in a soft and gentle way (23); and they just made a twiddle for E, because it came into the pictures so often (24); and they drew pictures of the sacred Beaver of the Tegumais for the B-sound (25, 26, 27, 28); and because it was a nasty,

25.   26.   27.   28.

nosy noise, they just drew noses for the N-sound, till they were tired (29); and they drew a picture of the big lake-pike's mouth for the greedy Ga-sound (30);

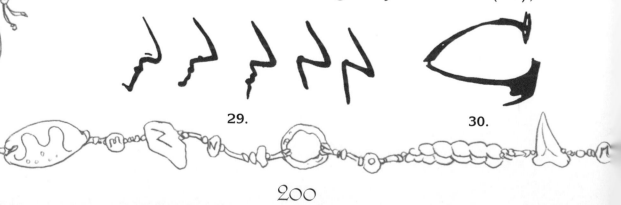

29.   30.

and they drew the pike's mouth again with a spear behind it for the scratchy, hurty Ka-sound (31); and they drew pictures of a little bit of the winding Wagai river for the nice windy-windy Wa-sound (32, 33); and so on and so forth and so following till they had done and drawn all the sound-pictures that they wanted, and there was the Alphabet, all complete.

31.

32.

33.

About the Author

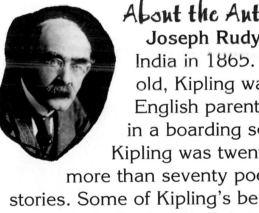

Joseph Rudyard Kipling was born in India in 1865. When he was six years old, Kipling was sent to England by his English parents where he was enrolled in a boarding school. By the time Kipling was twenty-five, he had published more than seventy poems, novels, and short stories. Some of Kipling's best-known works include *The Jungle Book, The Second Jungle Book, Kim,* and *Just So Stories.* In 1906, Kipling became the first English writer to be awarded the Nobel prize. Joseph Rudyard Kipling died in 1936.

SOMEDAY

from *Infinity Science Fiction*
by Isaac Asimov

**Perhaps the world will be like this
in years to come.
Perhaps people won't read and write.
Perhaps computers will do everything.**

Niccolo Mazetti lay stomach down on the rug, chin buried in the palm of one small hand, and listened to the Bard disconsolately. There was even the suspicion of tears in his dark eyes, a luxury an eleven-year-old could allow himself only when alone.

The Bard said, "Once upon a time in the middle of a deep wood, there lived a poor woodcutter and his two motherless daughters, who were each as beautiful as the day is long. The older daughter had long hair as black as a feather from a raven's wing, but the younger daughter had hair as bright and golden as the sunlight of an autumn afternoon.

"Many times while the girls were waiting for their father to come home from his day's work in the wood, the older girl would sit before a mirror and sing— —"

What she sang, Niccolo did not hear, for a call sounded from outside the room, "Hey, Nickie."

And Niccolo, his face clearing on the moment, rushed to the window and shouted, "Hey, Paul."

Paul Loeb waved an excited hand. He was thinner than Niccolo and not as tall, for all he was six months older. His face was full of repressed tension which showed itself most clearly in the rapid blinking of his eyelids. "Hey, Nickie, let me in. I've got an idea and a *half*. Wait till you hear it." He looked rapidly about him as though to check on the possibility of eavesdroppers, but the front yard was quite patently empty. He repeated, in a whisper, "Wait till you hear it."

"All right. I'll open the door."

The Bard continued smoothly, oblivious to the sudden loss of attention on the part of Niccolo. As Paul entered, the Bard was saying ". . . Thereupon, the lion said, 'If you will find me the lost egg of the bird which flies over the Ebony Mountain once every ten years, I will— —' "

Paul said, "Is that a Bard you're listening to? I didn't know you had one."

Niccolo reddened and the look of unhappiness returned to his face. "Just an old thing I had when I was a kid. It ain't much good." He kicked at the Bard with his foot and caught the scarred and discolored plastic covering a glancing blow.

The Bard hiccuped as its speaking attachment was jarred out of contact a moment, then it went on: "—for a year and a day until the iron shoes were worn out. The princess stopped at the side of the road. . ."

Paul said, "Boy, that *is* an old model," and looked at it critically.

Despite Niccolo's own bitterness against the Bard, he winced at the other's condescending tone. For the moment, he was sorry he had allowed Paul in, at least before he had restored the Bard to its usual resting place in the basement. It was only in the desperation of a dull day and a fruitless discussion with his father that he had resurrected it. And it turned out to be just as stupid as he had expected.

Nickie was a little afraid of Paul anyway, since Paul had special courses at school and everyone said he was going to grow up to be a Computing Engineer.

Not that Niccolo himself was doing badly at school. He got adequate marks in logic, binary manipulations, computing and elementary circuits: all the usual grammar-school subjects. But that was it! They were just the usual subjects and he would grow up to be a control-board guard like everyone else.

Paul, however, knew mysterious things about what he called electronics and theoretical mathematics and programing. Especially programing. Niccolo didn't even try to understand when Paul bubbled over about it.

Someday

Paul listened to the Bard for a few minutes and said, "You been using it much?"

"No!" said Niccolo, offended. "I've had it in the basement since before you moved into the neighborhood. I just got it out today— —" He lacked an excuse that seemed adequate to himself, so he concluded, "I just got it out."

Paul said, "Is that what it tells you about: woodcutters and princesses and talking animals?"

Niccolo said, "It's terrible. My dad says we can't afford a new one. I said to him this morning— —" The memory of the morning's fruitless pleadings brought Niccolo dangerously near tears, which he repressed in a panic. Somehow, he felt that Paul's thin cheeks never felt the stain of tears and that Paul would have only contempt for anyone else less strong than himself. Niccolo went on, "So I thought I'd try this old thing again, but it's no good."

Paul turned off the Bard, pressed the contact that led to a nearly instantaneous reorientation and recombination of the vocabulary, characters, plot lines and climaxes stored within it. Then he reactivated it.

The Bard began smoothly, "Once upon a time there was a little boy named Willikins whose mother had died and who lived with a stepfather and a stepbrother. Although the stepfather was very well-to-do, he begrudged poor Willikins the very bed he slept in so that Willikins was forced to get such rest as he could on a pile of straw in the stable next to the horses— —"

"Horses!" cried Paul.

"They're a kind of animal," said Niccolo. "I think."

"I know that! I just mean imagine stories about *horses.*"

"It tells about horses all the time," said Niccolo. "There are things called cows, too. You milk them but the Bard doesn't say how."

"Well, gee, why don't you fix it up?"

"I'd like to know how."

The Bard was saying, "Often Willikins would think that if only he were rich and powerful, he would show his stepfather and stepbrother what it meant to be cruel to a little boy, so one day he decided to go out into the world and seek his fortune."

Paul, who wasn't listening to the Bard, said, "It's *easy*. The Bard has memory cylinders all fixed up for plot lines and climaxes and things. We don't have to worry about that. It's just vocabulary we've got to fix so it'll know about computers and automation and electronics and real things about today. Then it can tell interesting stories, you know, instead of about princesses and things."

Niccolo said despondently, "I wish we could do that."

Paul said, "Listen, my dad says if I get into special computing school next year, he'll get me a *real* Bard, a late model. A big one with an attachment for space stories and mysteries. And a visual attachment, too!"

"You mean *see* the stories?"

"Sure, Mr. Daugherty at school says they've got things like that now, but not for just everybody. Only if I get into computing school, Dad can get a few breaks."

Niccolo's eyes bulged with envy. "Gee. *Seeing* a story."

"You can come over and watch anytime, Nickie."

"Oh, boy. Thanks."

"That's all right. But remember, I'm the guy who says what kind of story we get to hear."

"Sure. Sure." Niccolo would have agreed to much more onerous conditions.

Paul's attention returned to the Bard.

It was saying, " 'If that is the case,' said the king, stroking his beard and frowning till clouds filled the sky and lightning flashed, 'you will see to it that my entire land is freed of flies by this time day after tomorrow or— —' "

"All we've got to do," said Paul, "is open it up— —" He shut the Bard off again and was prying at its front panel as he spoke.

"Hey," said Niccolo, in sudden alarm. "Don't break it."

"I won't break it," said Paul impatiently. "I know all about these things." Then, with sudden caution, "Your father and mother home?"

"No."

"All right, then." He had the front panel off and peered in. "Boy, this is one of those one-cylinder things."

He worked away at the Bard's innards. Niccolo, who watched with painful suspense, could not make out what he was doing.

Paul pulled out a thin, flexible metal strip, powdered with dots. "That's the Bard's memory cylinder. I'll bet its capacity for stories is under a trillion."

"What are you going to do, Paul?" quavered Niccolo.

"I'll give it vocabulary."

"How?"

"Easy. I've got a book here. Mr. Daugherty gave it to me at school."

Paul pulled the book out of his pocket and pried at it till he had its plastic jacket off. He unreeled the tape a bit, ran it through the vocalizer, which he turned down to a whisper, then placed it within the Bard's vitals. He made further attachments.

"What'll that do?"

"The book will talk and the Bard will put it all on its memory tape."

"What good will that do?"

"Boy, you're a dope! This book is all about computers and automation and the Bard will get all the information. Then he can stop talking about kings making lightning when they frown."

Niccolo said, "And the good guy always wins anyway. There's no excitement."

"Oh, well," said Paul, watching to see if his setup was working properly, "that's the way they make Bards. They got to have the good guy win and make the bad guys lose and things like that. I heard my father talking about it once. He says that without censorship there'd be no telling what the younger generation would come to. He says it's bad enough as it is . . . There, it's working fine."

Paul brushed his hands against one another and turned away from the Bard. He said, "But listen, I didn't tell you my idea yet. It's the best thing you ever heard, I bet. I came right to you because I figured you'd come in with me."

"Sure, Paul, sure."

"Okay. You know Mr. Daugherty at school? You know what a funny kind of guy he is. Well, he likes me, kind of."

"I know."

"I was at his house after school today."

"You *were?*"

"Sure. He says I'm going to be entering computer school and he wants to encourage me and things like that. He says the world needs more people who can design advanced computer circuits and do proper programing."

"Oh?"

Paul might have caught some of the emptiness behind that monosyllable. He said impatiently, "Programing! I told you a hundred times. That's when you set up problems for the giant computers like Multivac to work on. Mr. Daugherty says it gets harder all the time to find people who can really run computers. He says anyone can keep an eye on the controls and check off answers and put through routine problems. He says the trick is to expand research and figure out ways to ask the right questions, and that's hard.

"Anyway, Nickie, he took me to his place and showed me his collection of old computers. He had tiny computers you had to push with your hand, with little knobs all over them. And he had a hunk of wood he called a slide rule with a little piece of it that went in and out. And some wires with balls on them. He even had a hunk of paper with a kind of thing he called a multiplication table."

Niccolo, who found himself only moderately interested, said, "A paper table?"

"It wasn't really a table like you eat on. It was different. It was to help people compute. Mr. Daugherty tried to explain but he didn't have much time and it was kind of complicated, anyway."

"Why didn't people just use a computer?"

"That was *before* they had computers," cried Paul.

"Before?"

"Sure. Do you think people always had computers? Didn't you ever hear of the cavemen?"

Niccolo said, "How'd they get along without computers?"

"*I* don't know. Mr. Daugherty says they just had children any old time and did anything that came into their heads whether it would be good for everybody or not. They didn't even know if it was good or not. And farmers grew things with their hands and people had to do all the work in the factories and run all the machines."

"I don't believe you."

"That's what Mr. Daugherty said. He said it was just plain messy and everyone was miserable . . . Anyway, let me get to my idea, will you?"

"Well, go ahead. Who's stopping you?" said Niccolo, offended.

"All right. Well, the hand computers, the ones with the knobs, had little squiggles on each knob. And the slide rule had squiggles on it. And the multiplication table was all squiggles. I asked what they were. Mr. Daugherty said they were numbers."

"What?"

"Each different squiggle stood for a different number. For 'one' you made a kind of mark, for 'two' you make another kind of mark, for 'three' another and so on."

"What for?"

"So you could compute."

"What *for?* You just tell the computer— —"

"Jiminy," cried Paul, his face twisting with anger, "can't you get it through your head? These slide rules and things didn't talk."

"Then how— —"

"The answers showed up in squiggles and you had to know what the squiggles meant. Mr. Daugherty says that, in olden days, everybody learned how to make squiggles when they were kids and how to decode them, too. Making squiggles was called 'writing' and decoding them was 'reading.' He says there was a different kind of squiggle for every word and they used to write whole books in squiggles. He said they had some at the museum and I could look at them if I wanted to. He said if I was going to be a real computer programer I would have to know about the history of computing and that's why he was showing me all these things."

Niccolo frowned. He said, "You mean everybody had to figure out squiggles for every word and *remember* them? . . . Is this all real or are you making it up?"

"It's all real. Honest. Look, this is the way you make a 'one.' " He drew his finger through the air in a rapid downstroke. "This way you make 'two,' and this way 'three.' I learned all the numbers up to 'nine.' "

Niccolo watched the curving finger uncomprehendingly. "But what's the good of it?"

"You can learn how to make words. I asked Mr. Daugherty how you made the squiggle for 'Paul Loeb' but he didn't know. He said there were people at the museum who would know. He said there were people who had learned how to decode whole books. He said computers could be designed to decode books and used to be used that way but not any more because we have real books now, with magnetic tapes that go through the vocalizer and come out talking, you know."

"Sure."

"So if we go down to the museum, we can get to learn how to make words in squiggles. They'll let us because I'm going to computer school."

Niccolo was riddled with disappointment. "Is that your idea? Holy Smokes, Paul, who wants to do that? Make stupid squiggles!"

"Don't you get it? Don't you *get* it? You dope. *It'll be secret message stuff!*"

"What?"

"Sure. What good is talking when everyone can understand you? With squiggles you can send secret messages. You can make them on paper and nobody in the world would know what you were saying unless they knew the squiggles, too. And they wouldn't, you bet, unless we taught them. We can have a real club, with initiations and rules and a clubhouse. Boy— —"

A certain excitement began stirring in Niccolo's bosom. "What kind of secret messages?"

"Any kind. Say I want to tell you to come over to my place and watch my new Visual Bard and I don't want any of the other fellows to come. I make the right squiggles on paper and I give it to you and you look at it and you know what to do. Nobody else does. You can even show it to them and they wouldn't know a thing."

"Hey, that's something!" yelled Niccolo, completely won over. "When do we learn how?"

"Tomorrow," said Paul. "I'll get Mr. Daugherty to explain to the museum that it's all right and you get your mother and father to say okay. We can go down right after school and start learning."

"Sure!" cried Niccolo. "We can be club officers."

"I'll be president," said Paul matter-of-factly. "You can be vice president."

"All right. Hey, this is going to be lots more fun than the Bard." He was suddenly reminded of the Bard and said in apprehension, "Hey, what about my old Bard?"

Paul turned to look at it. It was quietly taking in the slowly unreeling book, and the sound of the book's vocalizations was a dimly heard murmur.

He said, "I'll disconnect it."

He worked while Niccolo watched anxiously. After a few moments, Paul put his reassembled book into his pocket, replaced the Bard's panels and activated it.

The Bard said, "Once upon a time, in a large city, there lived a poor young boy named Fair Johnnie whose only friend in the world was a small computer. The computer, each morning, would tell the boy whether it would rain that day and answer any problems he might have. It was never wrong. But it so happened that one day the king of that land, having heard of the little computer, decided that he would have it as his own. With this purpose in mind, he called in his Grand Vizier and said— —"

Niccolo turned off the Bard with a quick motion of his hand. "Same old junk," he said passionately. "Just with a computer thrown in."

"Well," said Paul, "they got so much stuff on the tape already that the computer business doesn't show up much when random combinations are made. What's the difference, anyway? You just need a new model."

"We'll *never* be able to afford one. Just this dirty old miserable thing." He kicked at it again, hitting it more squarely this time. The Bard moved backward with a squeal of casters.

"You can always watch mine, when I get it," said Paul. "Besides, don't forget our squiggle club."

Niccolo nodded.

"I tell you what," said Paul. "Let's go over to my place. My father has some books about old times. We can listen to them and maybe get some ideas. You leave a note for your folks and maybe you can stay over for supper. Come on."

"Okay," said Niccolo, and the two boys ran out together. Niccolo, in his eagerness, ran almost squarely into the Bard, but he only rubbed at the spot on his hip where he had made contact and ran on.

The activation signal of the Bard glowed. Niccolo's collision closed a circuit and, although it was alone in the room and there was none to hear, it began a story, nevertheless.

But not in its usual voice somehow, in a lower tone that had a hint of throatiness in it. An adult, listening, might almost have thought that the voice carried a hint of passion in it, a trace of near feeling. But no one was listening.

The Bard said, "Once upon a time, there was a little computer named the Bard who lived all alone with cruel step-people. The cruel step-people continually made fun of the little computer and sneered at him, telling him he was good-for-nothing and that he was a useless object. They struck him and kept him in lonely rooms for months at a time.

"Yet through it all the little computer remained brave. He always did the best he could, obeying all orders cheerfully. Nevertheless, the step-people with whom he lived remained cruel and heartless.

"One day, the little computer learned that in the world there existed a great many computers of all sorts, great numbers of them. Some were Bards like himself, but some ran factories, and some ran farms. Some organized population and some analyzed all kinds of data. Many were very powerful and very wise, much more powerful and wise than the step-people who were so cruel to the little computer.

"And the little computer knew then that computers would always grow wiser and more powerful until someday-someday-someday— —"

But a valve must finally have stuck in the Bard's aging and corroding vitals, for as it waited alone in the darkening room through the evening, it could only whisper over and over again, "Someday-someday-someday."

About the Author

Isaac Asimov was born in Russia on January 2, 1920. When he was three years old, his family left Russia to start a new life in America. They arrived in New York City on February 3, 1923. Asimov took an early interest in books and by the age of five he had taught himself to read. Asimov was immediately attracted to science books. In school, Asimov skipped several grades and received a high school diploma at the age of fifteen. After graduating high school, the young Asimov went to Columbia University where he earned his Ph.D. in chemistry. He taught biochemistry at Boston College School of Medicine.

Although Asimov is best known for his science-fiction books, he also wrote children's books, articles, histories, and nonfiction science books. He won several awards including the Washington Post/Children's Book Guild Nonfiction Award. Asimov wrote nearly 500 books in his lifetime. Isaac Asimov died on April 6, 1992.

UNIT

6

A Changing America

There is a New America every morning when we wake up.
—Adlai E. Stevenson—

Escape from Slavery: The Boyhood of Frederick Douglass in His Own Words

Chapter One from *Escape from Slavery*
edited by Michael McCurdy

Introduction

Frederick Douglass was born in a small cabin near Hillsborough (now spelled Hillsboro), in Talbot County, Maryland, probably in 1817. He spent his early childhood on one of the thirteen farms that made up Edward Lloyd's immense wheat-producing plantation. Lloyd's chief manager, Aaron Anthony, was Frederick's first owner.

The cabin where Frederick lived was built of rough slabs of bark, with a floor made from the clay of nearby Tuckahoe Creek. As a small boy, he had no privacy in the cramped cabin that he shared with several cousins, two younger sisters, his grandparents Betsey and Isaac Bailey, and his grandmother's little son. To enable her daughters to work on the plantation, Betsey was expected to care for their children. She was a slave, but Isaac was a freeman. The family may originally have been brought from the West Indies to be sold to Maryland tobacco farmers.

Frederick's early years were relatively carefree. He explored the woods and creek around the cabin and enjoyed a loving home life. All this was to change abruptly when at the age of six he was sent to live in his owner's house. He accompanied his grandmother on the long walk, unaware of what was about to happen. Soon after their arrival, she left quietly, without Frederick knowing, until one of the children at his new home cried, "Fed, Fed! Grandmammy gone, Grandmammy gone!"

✧

I have no accurate knowledge of my age. By far the larger part of the slaves know as little of their ages as horses know of theirs, and it is the wish of most masters within my knowledge to keep their slaves thus ignorant. I do not remember to have ever met a slave who could tell of his birthday.

My mother was named Harriet Bailey. My father was a white man. The opinion was also whispered that my master was my father; but of the correctness of this opinion, I know nothing; the means of knowing was withheld from me. My mother and I were separated when I was but an infant.

I never saw my mother, to know her as such, more than four or five times in my life; and each of these times was very short in duration, and at night. She was hired by a Mr. Stewart, who lived about twelve miles from my home. She made her journeys to see me in the night, travelling the whole distance on foot, after the performance of her day's work. She was a field hand, and a whipping is the penalty of not being in the field at sunrise, unless a slave has special permission from his or her master to the contrary.

She was with me in the night. She would lie down with me, and get me to sleep, but long before I waked she was gone.

Very little communication ever took place between us. Death soon ended what little we could have while she lived, and with it her hardships and suffering. She died when I was about seven years old, on one of my master's farms, near Lee's Mill. I was not allowed to be present during her illness, at her death, or burial. She was gone long before I knew any thing about it. Never having enjoyed, to any considerable extent, her soothing presence, her tender and watchful care, I received the tidings of her death with much the same emotions I should have probably felt at the death of a stranger.

Men and women slaves received, as their monthly allowance of food, eight pounds of pork, or its equivalent in fish, and one bushel of corn meal. Their yearly clothing consisted of two coarse linen shirts, one pair of linen trousers, like the shirts, one jacket, one pair of trousers for winter, made of coarse negro cloth, one pair of stockings, and one pair of shoes; the whole of which could not have cost more than seven dollars.

The children unable to work in the field had neither shoes, stockings, jackets, nor trousers, given to them; their clothing consisted of two coarse linen shirts per year. When these failed them, they went naked. Children from seven to ten years old, of both sexes, almost naked, might be seen at all seasons of the year.

There were no beds given the slaves, unless one coarse blanket be considered such, and none but the men and women had these. They find less difficulty from the want of beds, than from the want of time to sleep; for when their day's work in the field is done, the most of them have their washing, mending, and cooking to do, and having few or none of the ordinary facilities for doing either of these, very many of their sleeping hours are consumed in preparing for the field the coming day; and when this is done, old and young, male and female, married and single, drop down side by side, on one common bed—the cold, damp floor— each covering himself or herself with their miserable blankets; and here they sleep till they are summoned to the field by the driver's horn.

At the sound of this, all must rise, and be off to the field. There must be no halting; every one must be at his or her post; and woe betides them who hear not this morning summons to the field; for if they are not awakened by the sense of hearing, they are by the sense of feeling; no age nor sex finds any favor. Mr. Severe, the overseer, used to stand by the door of the quarter, armed with a large hickory stick and heavy cowskin, ready to whip any one who was so unfortunate as not to hear, or, from any other cause, was prevented from being ready to start for the field at the sound of the horn.

Few privileges were esteemed higher, by the slaves of the out-farms, than that of being selected to do errands at the Great House Farm. While on their way, they would make the dense old woods, for miles around, reverberate with their wild songs. I did not, when a slave, understand the deep meaning of those rude and apparently incoherent songs. They told a tale of woe which was then altogether beyond my feeble comprehension; they were tones loud, long, and deep; they breathed the prayer and complaint of souls boiling over with the bitterest anguish. Every tone was a testimony against slavery, and a prayer to God for deliverance from chains.

I have often been utterly astonished, since I came to the north, to find persons who could speak of the singing, among slaves, as evidence of their contentment and happiness. It is impossible to conceive of a greater mistake. Slaves sing most when they are most unhappy. The songs of the slave represent the sorrows of his heart; and he is relieved by them, only as an aching heart is relieved by its tears. At least, such is my experience. I have often sung to drown my sorrow, but seldom to express my happiness. Crying for joy, and singing for joy, were alike uncommon to me while in the jaws of slavery. The singing of a man cast away upon a desolate island might be as appropriately considered as evidence of contentment and happiness, as the singing of a slave; the songs of the one and of the other are prompted by the same emotion.

I was not old enough to work in the field, and there being little else than field work to do, I had a great deal of leisure time. The most I had to do was to drive up the cows at evening, keep the fowls out of the garden, keep the front yard clean, and run of errands for my old master's daughter, Mrs. Lucretia Auld. The most of my leisure time I spent in helping Master Daniel Lloyd in finding his birds, after he had shot them. My connection with Master Daniel was of some advantage to me. He became quite attached to me, and was a sort of protector of me. He would not allow the older boys to impose upon me, and would divide his cakes with me.

Our food was coarse corn meal boiled. This was called *mush*. It was put into a large wooden tray or trough, and set down upon the ground. The children were then called, like so many pigs, and like so many pigs they would come and devour the mush; some with oyster-shells, others with pieces of shingle, some with naked hands, and none with spoons. He that ate fastest got most; he that was strongest secured the best place; and few left the trough satisfied.

I suffered much from hunger, but much more from cold. In hottest summer and coldest winter, I was kept almost naked—no shoes, no stockings, no jacket, no trousers, nothing on but a coarse tow linen shirt, reaching only to my knees. I had no bed. I must have perished with cold, but that, the coldest nights, I used to steal a bag which was used for carrying corn to the mill. I would crawl into this bag, and there sleep on the cold, damp, clay floor, with my head in and feet out. My feet have been so cracked with the frost, that the pen with which I am writing might be laid in the gashes.

About the Author

Frederick Douglass lived in slavery until September 1838. While working in Baltimore, Maryland, after a failed escape attempt, Douglass fled the city. After traveling by train and steamboat, Douglass finally arrived in New York City. Douglass became a leading spokesperson for the rights of African Americans and women. In 1845, his autobiography, *Narrative of the Life of Frederick Douglass, An American Slave,* was published. Shortly after, Douglass began a newspaper called *The North Star,* which later became known as the *Frederick Douglass' Papers.* When the Civil War began, Douglass was responsible for recruiting African Americans for the Union Army. He also served as Lincoln's advisor. Frederick Douglass continued advocating equality until his death on February 20, 1895.

Frederick Douglass

by Robert Hayden
from *Collected Poems of Robert Hayden*
edited by Frederick Glaysher

When it is finally ours, this freedom,
   this liberty, this beautiful
and terrible thing, needful to man
   as air,
usable as earth; when it belongs
   at last to all,
when it is truly instinct, brain matter,
   diastole, systole,
reflex action; when it is finally won;
   when it is more
than the gaudy mumbo jumbo
   of politicians:
this man, this Douglass, this former
   slave, this Negro
beaten to his knees, exiled, visioning
   a world
where none is lonely, none hunted,
   alien,
this man, superb in love and logic,
   this man
shall be remembered. Oh, not with
   statues' rhetoric,
not with legends and poems and
   wreaths of bronze alone,
but with the lives grown out of his life,
   the lives
fleshing his dream of the beautiful,
   needful thing.

Rails Across the Country

from *A History of US: Reconstruction and Reform*

by Joy Hakim

1 t was May 10, 1869, and hardly a person in the whole country didn't wish to be at Promontory Point in Utah. The people who were there listened to speeches, said a prayer, drank toasts (too many, so it was said), yelled, and cheered. Two brass bands blared. All over the country, newspapers held their presses so they could cover the grand event. The newspapers wouldn't tell the whole story—it would take years for the real story to be known—but when Leland Stanford (representing a railroad company that had laid tracks east from Sacramento, California, over the high and dangerous Sierra Nevada mountains and on to northern Utah)—when Leland Stanford shook hands with Thomas Durant (whose railroad company had laid tracks west from Omaha, Nebraska, over land the Indians thought they owned)—why, the whole country got excited. A telegraph operator, on a high pole above the crowd, sent out the message STAND BY, WE HAVE DONE PRAYING. Then Leland Stanford raised a silver hammer, whomped at a solid gold spike—and missed. No matter, the next swipe hit the nail on its head.

This all-time record was the result of a bet between two of the railroad owners. ∼

Five states had sent gold and silver spikes for this historic event, so the other bigwigs each got a chance to hammer away. When they were done, Chinese workmen quietly removed the fancy spikes and nailed regular ones in place. By that time the news had been sent to America's newspapers and people. TRANSCONTINENTAL RAILROAD COMPLETED. EAST AND WEST LINKED. In Philadelphia the Liberty Bell rang. Chicago held a parade that stretched for seven miles. In New York cannons blasted 100 times. You could now go by train from New York to California.

The building of that railroad had begun, in a way, on July 1, 1862, the day Abraham Lincoln signed the Pacific Railroad Act. There were visionaries—people with clear sight and imagination—who had talked even earlier of a railroad to cross the country. Lincoln's act got it started. But slowly. After all, there was a Civil War being fought. The country learned of the importance of railroads during that war, when armies were moved by train. But a railroad that stretched across the continent—that would have to wait until the war was over.

Leland Stanford leans against a hammer as the chief electrician F.L. Vandenburg, kneeling at Stanford's feet, adjusts a wire leading to the telegraph pole (top). A golden spike was removed from the track and replaced with a regular spike (left). ∿

Two companies built the railroad. The Central Pacific (starting in the West) and the Union Pacific (coming from the East). No one knew exactly where they would meet. It became a race—East against West. It was an important race for those who owned the railroad companies. The government was giving subsidies for each mile of railway track that was laid. So, of course, each side wanted to lay the most track.

Under the best conditions, laying track isn't easy. Conditions were rarely "best." Remember, this was frontier land they were crossing. The railroads had to bring all their supplies with them. If there was an emergency there was no place to go for help.

You lay tracks by putting heavy metal rails on top of wooden cross pieces—trimmed logs—called "ties." The Union Pacific used 40 railroad cars to haul the 400 tons of rails, timber, fuel, and food needed for each mile of track. The Central Pacific brought its rails, locomotives, and supplies from the East Coast on clipper ships that sailed around to Cape Horn at the tip of South America.

Laying tracks on flat land is not too difficult. But try crossing a mountain. You have a choice: you can go over or through. The railroad men did both of those things—they dug tunnels through some mountains and laid tracks over others. At first the equipment they used was about as fancy as what you might find in a neighbor's garage. Workers attacked rocks with pickaxes, they dug tunnels with shovels and their bare hands. They carried stones and dirt in wheelbarrows. Sometimes they used explosives; sometimes they blew themselves up.

The Central Pacific crews competed with the Union Pacific crews to lay the most track—until the government chose Promontory as the specific meeting place and settled the question. ⌒

Do you want to build a railroad, 19th-century style? Start with *graders:* men with picks, shovels, wheelbarrows, and wagons—they grade the land, making it as level as possible. Muscular *tracklayers* follow. They lift and place the heavy wooden ties and the heavier metal rails. Next come *gaugers, spikers,* and *bolters*—who get it all together and hammer the spikes in place. Each rail takes 10 spikes and each mile 400 rails.

The Central Pacific Railroad sent ships to China and brought 7,000 Chinese workers to California just to build the railroad. They paid them $1 a day. The Chinese worked incredibly hard, for long hours, and, mostly, were treated with contempt.

Coming the other way, on the Union Pacific, most workers were either ex-Confederate soldiers, former slaves, or Irish immigrants. They, too, worked hard. They lived in tent cities put up and taken down as the railroad went west. Those moving towns were tough, violent places where there was too much drinking and too many guns. There was constant fear of Indian raids.

The Indians—by treaty—had been guaranteed land west of the 95th meridian (a meridian is a line of longitude) as a permanent home. When the railroad got to Nebraska it was already at the 100th meridian. So Indians, understandably, were angered. They hated the thundering locomotives that were destroying the buffalo ranges. Native Americans raided the railroad camps, but not as often as the tales say. Indians didn't kill many trainmen; it was disease, accidents, avalanches, heat, and cold that were the worst killers. Some people deserved medals for what they accomplished—especially the engineers and organizers who arranged for the food and shelter, who planned the route, and who supervised the work. None of that was easy. They did it with incredible speed.

It is the winter of 1868, and Union Pacific crews have just crossed Wyoming's Green River in the shadow of Citadel Rock and the Wasatch range. On the other side of the mountains lie Utah, the Great Salt Lake, and Promontory Point. ⌒

   After the railroads met at Promontory Point, everyone had to wait two days to celebrate. That was because Thomas Durant was late. Union Pacific workmen had chained his fancy parlor-car train to some railroad track. They kept him hostage until he paid them overdue wages.

   By that time Durant was rich enough to make King Midas envious. So was Leland Stanford, who made his employees salute when he rode past in his private railroad car. When the transcontinental railroad was finished, Stanford, Durant, and the other railroad tycoons were national heroes. Today, many historians call them crooks.

Leland Stanford ꙩ

A private Pullman car. The rich could now travel in this style clear across the country. ꙩ

You see, they had asked for government aid in building the railroad. That was reasonable. It was too big an undertaking for individuals. They demanded more than money from the government; they wanted—and got—enormous and valuable land grants. That was greedy, but it wasn't illegal. Then they sold stock in their companies to the public, and got more money that way. That wasn't illegal, either. But when their companies gave out contracts for building the railroads, and those men in charge—Stanford, Durant, and company—took all the contracts for themselves, that was crooked. They didn't even share profits with their stockholders. That was really foul play. Worse than that, they charged the government twice what it actually cost to do the building. As you know, they hardly paid their workers. And, still worse, they allowed poor and unsafe workmanship, because it was cheaper and made their profits higher.

So that side of it was a mess, and when some of the story came out a few years later it created a big scandal. That was when U. S. Grant was president. It almost destroyed his term in office. All the fuss did help get laws passed to regulate business greed.

Grant himself (in straw hat and beard, hands on fence) came to settle a fight between Dodge the engineer (far left) and his railroad owner, Durant (in straw hat, to right of top-hatted man). Durant wanted Dodge to make the railroad even longer than it had to be so he could get more government subsidies. Dodge refused, and Grant backed him. ～

Still, to be fair, it took great imagination and some risk to finance the railroads. The men who did it had foresight and courage (even if they had no consideration for their employees, stockholders, or fellow citizens).

The good part of the story is that people in the United States could now travel from coast to coast in 10 days. Some people still went west in covered wagons, but it wouldn't be long before the wagons were history. Soon there were several transcontinental railroads. They were hauling things as well as people.

DISTANCES & ALTITUDES ON C.P.R.R.	MILES.	FEET.
San Francisco	0	0
Altamont	55	730
Lathrop	81	25
Sacramento	138	30
Cisco	230	593
Summit	243	70
Truckee	257	
Wadsworth	327	
Winnemucca	462	
Carlin	58	
Toano		
Promontory		
Ogden		

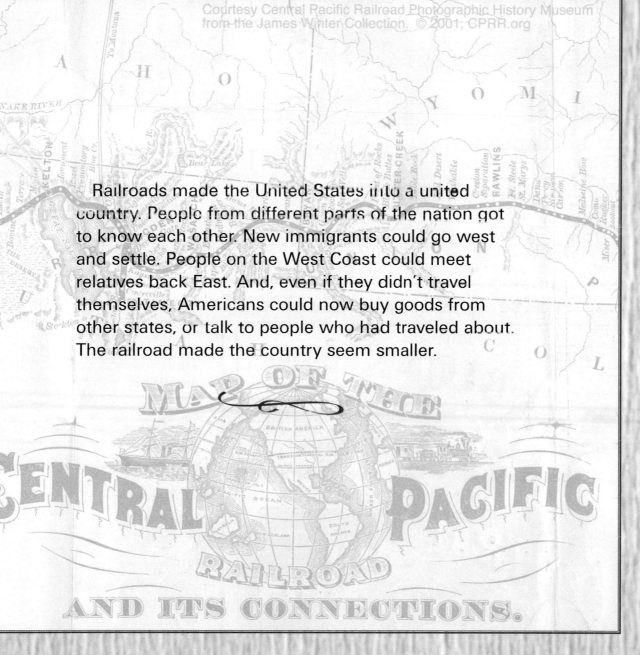

Railroads made the United States into a united country. People from different parts of the nation got to know each other. New immigrants could go west and settle. People on the West Coast could meet relatives back East. And, even if they didn't travel themselves, Americans could now buy goods from other states, or talk to people who had traveled about. The railroad made the country seem smaller.

I Hear America Singing

from *Leaves of Grass*
by Walt Whitman

I hear America singing, the varied carols I hear,
Those of mechanics, each one singing his as it should be
    blithe and strong,
The carpenter singing his as he measures his plank or beam,
The mason singing his as he makes ready for work, or leaves
    off work,
The boatman singing what belongs to him in his boat,
    the deckhand singing on the steamboat deck,
The shoemaker singing as he sits on his bench, the hatter
    singing as he stands,
The wood-cutter's song, the ploughboy's on his way in the
    morning, or at noon intermission or at sundown,
The delicious singing of the mother, or of the young wife at
    work, or of the girl sewing or washing,
Each singing what belongs to him or her and to none else,
The day what belongs to the day—at night the party of young
    fellows, robust, friendly,
Singing with open mouths their strong melodious songs.

July Hay. 1943. **Thomas Hart Benton.** Oil and egg tempera on composition board. 38" × 26¾". The Metropolitan Museum of Art, New York.

About the Author

Walt Whitman was born on the West Hills of Long Island, New York, on May 31, 1819. At the age of eleven, Whitman worked as a printer in New York City, then he began teaching at seventeen. In 1841 he embarked on a career as a journalist, quickly becoming editor for various papers in Brooklyn and New York. Whitman's firm beliefs in democracy and American ideals are most apparent in *Leaves of Grass,* a collection of twelve poems originally published in 1855. By the time of his death in 1892, Walt Whitman had added over 300 works to the original edition.

Glossary

Pronunciation Key

a as in **a**t	**o** as in **o**x	**ou** as in **ou**t	**ch** as in **ch**air
ā as in l**a**te	**ō** as in r**o**se	**u** as in **u**p	**hw** as in **wh**ich
â as in c**a**re	**ô** as in b**o**ught	**ū** as in **u**se	**ng** as in ri**ng**
ä as in f**a**ther	and r**a**w	**ûr** as in t**ur**n,	**sh** as in **sh**op
e as in s**e**t	**oi** as in c**oi**n	g**er**m, l**ear**n,	**th** as in **th**in
ē as in m**e**	**o͞o** as in b**oo**k	f**ir**m, w**or**k	**t͟h** as in **th**ere
i as in **i**t	**o͞o** as in t**oo**	**ə** as in **a**bout,	**zh** as in trea**s**ure
ī as in k**i**te	**or** as in f**or**m	chick**e**n, penc**i**l,	
		cann**o**n, circ**u**s	

The mark (ˊ) is placed after a syllable with a heavy accent, as in **chicken** (chik´ ən).

The mark (ˊ) after a syllable shows a lighter accent, as in **disappear** (dis´ ə pēr ´).

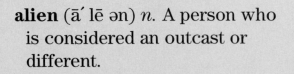

alien (ā´ lē ən) *n*. A person who is considered an outcast or different.

amiably (ā´ mē ə blē) *adv*. In a friendly and kindly manner.

amulet (am´ yə lət) *n*. A charm usually worn around the neck to protect the wearer.

annihilation (ə nī´ ə lā´ shən) *n*. The state of being completely wiped out or destroyed.

antihistamine (an´ tē his´ tə mēn´) *n*. A drug used to counteract allergic reactions.

ardor (är´ dər) *n*. Strong enthusiasm or devotion.

assurances (ə shûr´ əns əz) *n*. Statements supposed to make one certain; without doubt.

babushkas (bə bo͞osh´ kəs) *n*. Scarves folded triangularly and worn on women's heads.

baracholka (bâr ə khol´ kə) *n.* Type of market.

bard (bärd) *n.* A poet who wrote and narrated verses about leaders and heroes.

barometer (bə ro´ mə tər) *n.* An instrument used to measure atmospheric pressure and to predict changes in the weather.

baron (bar´ ən) *n.* The lowest rank of a nobleman in Great Britain.

bedraggled (bi dra´ gəld) *adj.* Wet and dirty as if trailed through mud.

begrudged (bi grujd´) *v.* Gave unwillingly and with displeasure.

benignant (bi nig´ nənt) *adj.* Kind and compassionate.

betides (bi tīds) *v.* To take place.

bigwigs (big´ wigs´) *n. Slang.* Important people.

blithe (blīth) *adj.* Lighthearted and happy.

booby (boo´ bē) *n.* A person considered foolish or unthinking.

brinza (brin´ za) *n.* A type of goat cheese similar to feta.

Bubbe (boo´ bē) *n.* Yiddish, "Grandmother."

bushel (boo´ shəl) *n.* A measure for dry goods; a bushel is equal to 32 quarts.

canter (kan´ tər) *n.* The stride of a horse, faster than a trot but slower than a gallop. [After *Canterbury*, England. The believed pace of pilgrims riding to Canterbury.]

casters (kas´ tərs) *n.* Small wheels that swivel, usually found underneath heavy objects to make them easier to move.

cavity (ka´ və tē) *n.* A hole or hollow place.

censorship (sen´ sər ship´) *n.* The act of examining books, films, or other material to remove what is considered morally, politically, or otherwise objectionable. [Latin *censor*, Roman *censor*, from *censere*, "to assess."]

chaplain (cha´ plən) *n.* A clergy member who leads services and counseling for a military unit. [Medieval Latin, *chapel.*]

Chickahominy (chi´ kə hä´ mə nē) *n.* A river located in Virginia. Many fights occurred along its banks during the Civil War.

commissions (kə mi´ shəns) *n.*
Tasks given to a person to do.

communal (kə myoo´ nəl) *adj.*
Public; shared by all.

conceive (kən sēv´) *v.* To imagine
or to form an idea. [Middle
English, from Latin *concipere*,
"to take in."]

concoction (kən kok´ shən) *n.*
Something made up of a
combination of things.

condescending (kon´ di sen´ ding)
adj. Having a superior attitude.

contempt (kən tempt´) *n.* A
feeling of disrespect or scorn
toward a person.

convulsively (kən vul´ siv lē)
adv. With intense, involuntary
muscular contractions. [Latin,
convellere, convuls-, "to pull
violently."]

copse (kops) *n.* A thick area of
small trees and shrubs.

cossacks (ko´ saks) *n.* Members
of a group in southern Russia
classified as cavalry in the
czarist army.

countenance (koun´ tən əns) *n.*
A look of support or approval.

coverlid (kuv´ ər lid) *n.* A
bedspread.

crescent (kre´ sənt) *n.* A thin,
curved shape.

D

delirium (di lir´ ē əm) *n.* A state of
confusion caused by a high fever.
[Latin *delirare*, "to be crazy."]

despondent (di spän´ dənt)
adj. Showing or feeling
discouragement.

devoured (di vourd´) *v.* Ate
greedily. [Latin *devorare*: *de-* +
vorare, "to swallow."]

Diaspora (dī as´ pə rə) *n.* A
community of people separated
from their original homeland.
[Greek, from *diaspeirein*, "to
scatter."]

diastole (dī as´ tə lē) *n.* The
rhythmic expansion of the heart's
cavities when they fill with blood.
[Greek *diastellein*, "to expand."]

disconsolately (dis kon´ sə lət lē) *adv.* In a gloomy, cheerless way.

disease-laden (di zēz´ lā´ dən) *adj.* Carrying or filled with disease.

docile (do´ sīl´) *adj.* Easy to handle.

eaves (ēvz) *n.* The lower part of a roof that overhangs the wall.

engrossing (in grō´ sing) *adj.* Taking all of one's attention; absorbing.

equine (ē´ kwīn´) *adj.* Of, relating to, or characteristic of a horse.

esteemed (is tēmd´) *v.* Thought highly of.

exiled (ek´ sīld´) *v.* To have sent a person away from his or her home or country as punishment.

fervent (fûr´ vənt) *adj.* Showing great emotion.

festered (fes´ tərd) *v.* To have caused increasing aggravation.

flints (flints) *n.* Hard stones that produce sparks when struck. [Old High German *flins*, "pebble, stone."]

foresight (fōr´ sīt´) *n.* Good judgment in planning for the future.

fruitless (frōōt´ ləs) *adj.* Unsuccessful; useless.

gaping (gāp´ ing) *v.* Staring at in amazement.

Grand Vizier (grand´ və zir´) *n.* A high officer of various Muslim countries.

grande dame (grän´ däm´) *n.* A woman of great authority or stature. [French, "great lady."]

gypsum (jip´ səm) *n.* A colorless, white, or yellowish mineral used in the manufacture of plaster of paris, various plaster products, and fertilizer.

haunches (hônch´ əz) *n.* The hip and upper thigh of a body.

heft (heft) *v.* To lift in order to estimate weight. [From 15th century *heave*, after pairs such as *weave, weft*.]

heiress (âr´ əs) *n.* A woman who received money or property from a person after that person's death.

Pronunciation Key: at; lāte; câre; fäther; set; mē; it; kīte; ox; rōse; ô in bought; coin; book; too; form; out; up; ūse; tûrn; ə sound in about, chicken, pencil, cannon, circus; chair; hw in which; ring; shop; thin; there; zh in treasure

herring (hâr´ ing) *n.* A small saltwater fish found in the northern Atlantic Ocean that can be eaten smoked, fresh, or canned.

hides (hīds) *n.* The tough, thick skins of animals.

hurricanes (hûr´ ə kāns´) *n.* Storms with heavy rains and strong winds. [Spanish *huracán*, after *Huracán*, the wind god of the Carib people.]

ignorant (ig´ nə rənt) *adj.* Uninformed or unaware.

imminent (i´ mə nənt) *adj.* About to occur.

imperceptibly (im´ pər sep´ tə blē) *adv.* In a way that is impossible or difficult to observe with the mind or senses.

impose (im pōz´) *v.* To force or make unfair demands on a person.

incoherent (in´ kō hir´ ənt) *adj.* Not clear.

inexplicable (i´ nik spli´ kə bəl) *adj.* Difficult or impossible to explain.

ingested (in jes´ təd) *v.* To have taken into the body through the mouth. [Latin *ingestus*, past participle of *ingerere*, "to carry in."]

inoculation (i nä´ kyə lā´ shən) *n.* The act of introducing a substance, such as a vaccine, into the body to produce immunity to a specific disease.

intermission (in´ tər mi´ shən) *n.* A breaking or stopping point between activities.

intrigued (in trēgd´) *v.* Interested.

invalid (in´ və ləd) *n.* A person unable to care for him- or herself due to injury or illness. [Latin *invalidus*, "weak."]

jostle (jo´ səl) *v.* To move and crash together as a result of being crowded together.

Kazakhs (kə zäks´) *n.* Members of a Turkic people inhabiting Kazakhstan and parts of China.

keening (kēn´ ing) *v.* Wailing loudly, expressing grief for the dead.

larvae (lär´ vē) *n.* Newly hatched, wormlike forms of insects before transformation through other stages of growth.

lee (lē) *n.* A covered or sheltered area.

legitimate (li ji´ tə mət) *adj.* Based on accepted standards; reasonable.

leisure (lē´ zhər) *n.* Free time to do what one enjoys.

mason (mā´ sən) *n.* A person who builds with bricks, stones, or cement.

matron (mā´ trən) *n.* A dignified married woman.

mean (mēn) *adj.* Shabby; in poor condition.

merciful (mûr´ si fəl) *adj.* Showing great kindness or forgiveness beyond expectations.

morbid (mor´ bəd) *adj.* Frightful or awful.[Latin *morbus*, "disease."]

mulled (muld) *v.* To have considered or pondered extensively in one's mind.

mumbo jumbo (mum´ bō jum´ bō) *n.* Gibberish; unclear language. [*Mumbo Jumbo*, a masked individual among Mandingo peoples of western Africa.]

mustard-plaster (mus´ tərd plas´ tər) *n.* A paste-like mixture (containing mustard) that hardens when dry; applied to the body to help healing.

ninepence (nīn´ pens) *n.* An old English coin; "nine pennies."

notion (nō´ shən) *n.* A belief.

obliged (ə blījd´) *v.* To be made thankful for a service or favor.

oblivious (ə bli´ vē əs) *adj.* Not aware or mindful of.

obstinately (ob´ stə nət lē) *adv.* Unwilling to change one's mind; in a stubborn way.

> **Pronunciation Key: at**; l**ā**te; c**â**re; f**ä**ther; s**e**t; m**ē**; **i**t; k**ī**te; **o**x; r**ō**se; **ô** in b**ou**ght; c**oi**n; b**oo**k; t**oo**; f**or**m; **ou**t; **u**p; **ū**se; t**û**rn; **ə** sound in **a**bout, chick**e**n, penc**i**l, cann**o**n, circ**u**s; **ch**air; **hw** in **wh**ich; ri**ng**; **sh**op; **th**in; **th**ere; **zh** in trea**s**ure

onerous (o´ nə rəs) *adj.* Troublesome or burdensome.

ornate (or nāt´) *adj.* Having much decoration.

ostentatiously (os´ tən tā´ shəs lē) *adv.* In a showy way that draws attention.

panacea (pa´ nə sē´ ə) *n.* A cure for all things. [Latin, from Greek *panakēs*, "all-healing."]

patently (pa´ tənt lē) *adv.* Plainly or clearly.

peculiar (pi kyōōl´ yər) *adj.* Strange; unusual.

pensively (pen´ siv lē) *adv.* To express with melancholy thoughtfulness.

perturbed (pər tûrbd´) *adj.* Upset or anxious. [Middle English, from Latin *perturbare*, "to throw into confusion," from *per-* + *turbare*, "to disturb."]

plaques (pläks) *n.* Scaly patches formed on the skin.

pommel (po´ məl) *n.* The front part of a saddle. [Vulgar Latin *pomellum*, "ball, knob."]

pooh-poohed (pōō´ pōōd´) *v. Informal.* Dismissed; made light of.

proprietary (prə prī´ ə ter´ ē) *adj.* Owned under a trademark or patent, as a drug. [From Latin *proprietas*, "property."]

prowl (proul) *v.* To move quietly or secretly.

purging (pûrj´ ing) *v.* Emptying of the bowels.

quavering (kwā´ vər ing) *v.* Trembling. [Middle English *quaven*, "to tremble."]

random (ran´ dəm) *adj.* Made or done with no clear pattern; made or done by chance.

ravishing (ra´ vi shing) *adj.* Very appealing or captivating.

redoubled (rē du´ bəld) *v.* Doubled; repeated.

regulate (re′ gyə lāt′) *v.* To manage or control. [Middle English, from Latin *regula*, "rule."]

render (ren′ dər) *v.* To cause to become; make.

resilient (ri zil′ yənt) *adj.* Ability to recover easily or return to original shape or position.

resurrected (re′ zə rek′ təd) *v.* To be brought back into use.

reverberate (ri vûr′ bə rāt′) *v.* To repeat or echo a sound.

rhetoric (re′ tə rik) *n.* Language that is elaborate or embellished.

robust (rō bust′) *adj.* Having strength and energy. [Latin *robustus*, "oaken, strong."]

romps (romps) *v.* To play in a lively manner.

rosary (rō′ zə rē) *n.* A string of beads on which prayers are counted. [Middle English, "rose garden," from Medieval Latin *rosarium*, "rose garden, rosary."]

rubles (rōō′ bəls) *n.* The basic unit of money in Russia. [Possibly from Old Russian *rubli*, "cut piece" (a piece cut from wood).]

rude (rōōd) *adj.* Unpolished; primitive.

rummaged (ru′ mijd) *v.* To have looked for something by moving things around.

saliva (sə lī′ və) *n.* A clear liquid found in the mouth; produced by glands in the mouth to keep the mouth moist and to help in chewing and digestion.

sandbar (sand′ bär) *n.* A mound of sand that has been built up by waves in a river or in coastal waters.

scourge (skûrj) *n.* A source of widespread suffering and devastation such as that caused by an epidemic or war.

secrete (si krēt′) *v.* To release a chemical substance into the body.

shalom (shä lōm′) *interj.* A traditional Jewish greeting or good-bye.

silhouette (si′ lə wet′) *n.* The dark outline of a figure or object. [French, after Étienne de *Silhouette* (1709-1767), French finance minister.]

Pronunciation Key: at; lāte; câre; fäther; set; mē; it; kīte; ox; rōse; ô in bought; coin; bŏŏk; tōō; form; out; up; ūse; tûrn; ə sound in about, chicken, pencil, cannon, circus; chair; hw in which; ring; shop; thin; there; zh in treasure

sop (sop) *n.* Food soaked in a liquid.

spasms (spa´ zəms) *n.* Sudden, involuntary contractions of a muscle or group of muscles.

spavins (spa´ vəns) *n.* Bony enlargements of joints on horses' hind legs; often associated with strain.

spellbound (spel´ bound´) *adj.* Held by another as if under an incantation, or spell.

steppe (step) *n.* A vast grass-covered plain, as found in southeast Europe and Asia.

stock (stok´) *n.* Shares in the ownership of a company.

subsidies (sub´ sə dēz) *n.* Financial assistance given to a person or group by the government in support of a project. [Middle English, from Latin *subsidium*, "support, assistance."]

surplus (sûr´ plus) *n.* An amount greater than needed. [Medieval Latin *superplus*, "more."]

sustain (sə stān´) *v.* To maintain. [From Latin *sustinēre*, "to hold up."]

syringe (sə rinj´) *n.* A medical instrument used to inject fluids into the body or draw them from the body.

systole (sis´ tə lē) *n.* The rhythmic contraction of the heart. [Greek *systolē*, from *systellein*, "to contract."]

T

testimony (tes´ tə mō´ nē) *n.* A statement.

tethered (te´ thərd) *v.* To have fastened or held an animal in place with a rope or chain.

theoretical (thē´ ə re´ ti kəl) *adj.* Of, related to, or based on theory.

tide (tīd) *n.* The rise and fall of the sea's surface.

tidings (tī´ dings) *n.* Information or news.

tubers (tōō´ bərs) *n.* Thick stems of plants found underground.

tycoons (tī kōōns´) *n.* Wealthy businesspeople.

undertaking (un´ dər tā´ king) *n.*
A task or venture.

vanity (va´ nə tē) *n.* Too much
pride in one's appearance.

vapors (vā´ pərs) *n.* Thin steam or
smoke that can be seen in the air.

venison (ve´ nə sən) *n.* The meat
of a deer used as food. [Middle
English, from Old French
veneison, "hunting, game."]

ventured (ven´ chərd) *v.* To have
undertaken a new situation with
a doubtful outcome. [Middle
English *venteren*, from *aventure*,
"adventure."]

vigil (vi´ jəl) *n.* The act of keeping
watch over. [Late Latin *vigilia*,
from Latin, "wakefulness, watch,"
from *vigil*, "awake."]

vintage (vin´ tij) *n.* The grapes
or wine produced in a vineyard.

whittling (hwit´ ling) *v.* Cutting
small pieces from a portion of
wood using a knife.

winced (winsd) *v.* Moved suddenly
or involuntarily, as in pain or
distress.